Praise for *One-Minute Mindfulness*

"This is a book [you] can pick up and start using right away. The 50 Simple Ways are truly small, simple changes that can be easily incorporated in people's lives, one day at a time."

— Anna Jedrziewski, *New Age Retailer*

Praise for Donald Altman's *The Mindfulness Code*

"*The Mindfulness Code* can greatly enhance the ability of anyone to live with a greater sense of direction and self-control."

— Jeffrey M. Schwartz, MD, coauthor of *The Mind & the Brain*

"An antidote to the stress and hurriedness of modern life. In an age where we are pushed to perform ever better, Donald Altman reminds us that kindness, acceptance, and listening — just listening — are as admirable and transformative as any work or monetary achievement."

— Robert Biswas-Diener, coauthor of *Happiness*

"This well-written book addresses the root problems in anybody's life, and Altman's suggestions will certainly prove beneficial to readers who follow them."

— Bhante Henepola Gunaratana,
author of *Mindfulness in Plain English*

"*The Mindfulness Code* is a wonderful mix of warmth, humor, and gentle wisdom. Donald Altman weaves an engrossing blend of insights and personal stories from his many years as a skilled therapist along with illustrative research findings and many helpful mindfulness exercises. This book will hand you the keys for unlocking a life of greater ease and happiness."

— Zen Roshi Jan Chozen Bays, MD,
author of *Mindful Eating* and *A Year of Mindful Living*

"*The Mindfulness Code* is like having your own personal mindfulness coach. Altman's joy, passion, and knowledge are evident in each of the book's clearly written experiential teachings. This book cannot help but bring more joy, happiness, and contentment to the lives of everyone who reads it. It is a much-needed elixir for these turbulent times."

— Randall Fitzgerald, author of *The Hundred-Year Lie*
and former roving editor for *Reader's Digest*

"Donald Altman's latest book is a feast of kindness, wisdom, humor, and insight. Each chapter offers practical and inspiring ways to cultivate inner peace amid everyday life.... Once you start cracking *The Mindfulness Code*, you won't want to stop."

— Ronna Kabatznick, PhD, assistant clinical professor at
Langley Porter Psychiatric Institute,
University of California, San Francisco

"For those looking for more meaning from work or at work, *The Mindfulness Code* opens the door to discovering how you can derive more satisfaction from what you do. Happiness, as Altman explains, can come from what you do for yourself as well as for others.... You will find yourself reaching for [it] again and again as you explore meaning in your own life's work."

— John Baldoni, author of *Lead Your Boss* and *Lead by Example*

"*The Mindfulness Code* is an open-source secret of mindful living, a compassionate invitation to infuse mindfulness into every aspect of one's life. In offering a set of four keys for overcoming suffering, Altman remains an ever-skillful locksmith, narrating an innovative existential map with the help of teachings, inspirations, clinical vignettes, personal revelations, and ready-to-use techniques."

— Pavel Somov, PhD, author of
Present Perfect: Letting Go of Perfectionism and the Need to Control

"*The Mindfulness Code* richly integrates ancient body-mind-spirit knowledge with cutting-edge brain science. The book is filled with evidence-based research practices designed to relieve suffering caused by anxiety, depression, and life difficulties. Individuals and therapists alike will benefit from these simple, realistic, and achievable tools."

— Greg Crosby, MA, LPC, CGP, trainer, psychotherapist,
and faculty member at Portland State University
and Marylhurst University

one-minute
mindfulness

ALSO BY DONALD ALTMAN

Art of the Inner Meal

Living Kindness

Meal by Meal

The Mindfulness Code

one-minute
mindfulness

50 Simple Ways to Find Peace, Clarity,
and New Possibilities in a Stressed-Out World

DONALD ALTMAN

New World Library
Novato, California

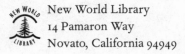 New World Library
14 Pamaron Way
Novato, California 94949

The material in this book is intended for education. It is not meant to take the place of diagnosis and treatment by a qualified medical practitioner or therapist. No expressed or implied guarantee as to the effects of the use of the recommendations can be given nor liability taken. The author's experiences used as examples throughout this book are true, although identifying details such as name and location have been changed to protect the privacy of others.

Text design by Tona Pearce Myers

Library of Congress Cataloging-in-Publication Data
Altman, Don, date.
 One-minute mindfulness : 50 simple ways to find peace, clarity, and new possibilities in a stressed-out world / Donald Altman.
    p.   cm.
Includes bibliographical references and index.
ISBN 978-1-60868-030-6 (pbk. : alk. paper)
1. Meditation. 2. Stress (Psychology) 3. Mind and body. I. Title.
BF637.M4A46 2011
158.1'2—dc23   2011023546

First printing, August 2011
ISBN 978-1-60868-030-6
Printed in Canada on 100% postconsumer-waste recycled paper

New World Library is a proud member of the Green Press Initiative.

10 9 8 7 6 5 4 3 2 1

*This book is dedicated to peace
and all who seek peace,
within and without.*

Contents

Part 2
One-Minute Mindfulness for Work and Creativity

Part 3
One-Minute Mindfulness for Relationships and Love

Part 4
One-Minute Mindfulness for Health and Well-Being

Part 5
One-Minute Mindfulness for Nature, Spirituality, and Contemplation

Introduction

*I*f there is a single secret to one-minute mindfulness, it is this: live the next sixty seconds as if your whole life depended on them, with a sense of urgency and excitement, or as if you had just arrived in a foreign land where there is nothing expected, hackneyed, or taken for granted. This is a journey into life's true possibility, freshness, mystery, wonder, and novelty. After all, who knows what amazing things may happen in the next minute? *One-Minute Mindfulness* offers the empowering perspective that how you think and act in the upcoming minute, and the next, determines nothing less than your experience of life.

The choice for a joy-filled life is waiting for you, and it is much closer than you think because an untapped wealth of being already lies within you. There are many different definitions for wealth, and many measure the static or material aspects of life. But only spiritual and psychological wealth give you the ability to be truly alive and to experience a greater degree of control over your life than you may have ever imagined. One-minute mindfulness realigns your life by letting you break free from automatic mode, giving you the freedom to choose how to respond to life's difficult, intolerable, and impossible situations.

This is wealth that enhances situations and moments that are ripe and ready to be awakened with joy, meaning, and possibility, but that otherwise you may have ignored. Believe it or not, this is a process that transforms your life into one of openness, joy, peace, patience, and presence. It all depends on how you choose to encounter each minute. Sound impossible? Read on, and you'll discover that it isn't. One-minute mindfulness will help you reconnect with those precious times when you believed *anything* was possible, when you lived in the present moment, fully and completely. Recovering that lost capability is easier than you think.

How would your life change if you were to recognize that all your worries, anxieties, and fears are ingrained habits of thought and behavior? What if you were to realize that the past and the future are merely mirages of the mind? The truth is we have a choice, and what is more, whether we seize or squander the choice to be fully alive depends on how we engage in the next sixty seconds. If you feel you are always running behind and busy making predictions about what will or should happen, if you are unceasingly worried and anxious about the future or unduly preoccupied with the past, or if you feel life is passing you by and you're not connecting with others in a meaningful way, one-minute mindfulness will help you to reinvigorate your life in a nurturing way that lets you come back to your senses. In doing so, you will unlock each minute's potential to make the difference between feeling acceptance, fulfillment, and happiness and feeling resistance, dissatisfaction, and unhappiness.

What more could we ask for than to have this choice? Of course, this does not mean you will win the next Powerball lottery (sorry about that) or life's jackpot and have all your problems solved in the next sixty seconds. But if there is any joy, gratitude, or appreciation to be found in life, there is no better place to locate it than right here and now by bringing an open heart and compassion to all the uninvited visitors that inevitably enter your life — the good, the bad, the ugly, the boring, the unpleasant, the despicable, the habitual, the blissful. When you become skillful with your awareness in present time, you will find that acceptance brings an amazingly powerful and positive outcome for even an unwelcome life obstacle.

One-minute mindfulness is actually a human birthright, an innate "sense-ability." Our natural ability to be fully present, however, is being challenged and is in danger of being lost. Technology's onslaught of nonstop information is splintering our attention and recalibrating our brains to "future think" — a future-oriented collective mind-set that emphasizes virtual relationships, preoccupation with the future, and activities that disorient and forfeit the present moment. Although our culture of technology and future think provides many benefits — including a greater diversity of information, speed in communication, and freedom from being tied to a single location — its complexity also demands more of our attentional bandwidth, creates an ongoing learning curve, and favors, obviously, a future orientation. One-minute mindfulness is not "antitechnology." Technology and future planning grant us tremendous benefits. But regardless of how hard we plan for tomorrow, the balance we need to locate life's fundamental goodness is found in the next sixty seconds.

With one-minute mindfulness, we discover a direct and simple path back to our lives in the fullest sense — even in a culture of technology. Mindfulness is a form of awareness and attention that enables us to peer into the truth of this moment. Mindfulness is not about the fleeting hedonistic satisfaction we get from filling up on material stuff, though it is about relishing the price-less treasures of experience and relationship that occur in the immediate moment.

Embracing the path of one-minute mindfulness is not with-out change; in fact, this path embraces the essence of change. It requires, for example, that you question worldviews you cur-rently hold that may be limiting or unbeneficial. Consider how normal it is for us to compare ourselves to machines. In the past hundred years, we have come to view ourselves increasingly in mechanical terms. You can explore this view right now by answering the following three questions:

1. In the past week, have you in some way felt good or bad about your capacity to accomplish, to be efficient and productive?

2. In the past week, did you eat two or more meals while also working — for example, while being on the com-puter, during a business lunch, or while doing another task, whether at work or at home?

3. In the past week, did you more than twice sacrifice sleep to get more work done, lose sleep worrying about work, or use a stimulant such as caffeine to give yourself energy to work harder?

If you answered yes to two or more of these questions, you may well be viewing yourself with a machinelike mind-set, even though you are not a machine to be manipulated for greater efficiency and productivity. How often do you think of food as "fuel for your engine" and miss out on the opportunity to savor the fla-vors and social connections food offers? For us to fully inhabit each minute, it is important that we examine and let go of such limiting mind-sets.

Recently, when I described one-minute mindfulness to a

friend, he thought it sounded like a lot of work. His exact words were, "That sounds exhausting, having to work at each minute!" We laughed, and I assured him that anyone practicing one-minute mindfulness will inevitably zone out. But I also explained that one-minute mindfulness is really about mining the treasure hidden in every moment — and the more we find joy, novelty, and fulfillment in the next minute, the more likely we are to continue to commit ourselves to the practice.

I hope you will approach this book as a journey of discovery. The pages that follow serve as a gentle guide, directing you to become more awake and aware throughout your day of the possibilities present in every sixty seconds. *One-Minute Mindfulness* contains examples, anecdotes, and observations that come from my experience as a psychotherapist and as a Buddhist monk. The book also looks at leading-edge brain research that shows how adaptable we are at rewiring established neuronal networks. Mostly, though, *One-Minute Mindfulness* is a practical book about consciously participating in the next sixty seconds of your life. It is part guidebook and part workbook for making this moment count. Each chapter contains an exercise or practice for building awareness and centering attention. The awareness exercises are meant to help you touch this moment — which can be harder than it seems. As a mindfulness student once said to his teacher, "Every time I start to think about how I'm finally in the here and now, I realize the moment has already passed."

The good news is that the effort is well worth it. According to Buddhist psychology, mindfulness is a path to enlightenment. I take that to mean that by fostering a curious, compassionate, and openhearted awareness in each moment, we can be blessed with clarity, joy, peace, love, and wisdom while also reducing our suffering and the suffering of others. To be alive is to totally and openly participate in the simplicity and elegance of here and now. A total commitment to the present moment is as close as the tip of your nose and the tips of your fingers. Now is when you take that all-important next inhalation and experience the blessings of the body. Only in this minute can the pink dawn of the morning's light stimulate your retinas. It's in this moment that you connect with another person's smile or touch.

This book is organized into five parts to help you integrate one-minute mindfulness into the various aspects of daily life. Part 1, "One-Minute Mindfulness for Home and Play," shows you how to bring more awareness to your home life, from the early morning hours to the final moments before you go to bed. You will learn to retrain your brain, to step out of automatic mode, and to find the nurturing moments that make each day worthwhile and memorable. You may be surprised to find out how much joy is waiting for you in ways and places you never before considered.

Part 2, "One-Minute Mindfulness for Work and Creativity," illustrates that it isn't necessary to view yourself or your work mechanically in order to be productive or creative. Here is where you will learn to apply new perspectives of gratitude and purpose in the workplace. Engaging in your livelihood in a new way can bring optimism and new energy to what you do and how you do it. The exercises will show you how to move away from perfectionism and toward the process of the next minute, where you will find more fulfillment and excitement while still being highly effective.

Part 3, "One-Minute Mindfulness for Relationships and Love," offers tools for healing relationships sixty seconds at a time. The next minute can be an alchemical moment that reveals the gold hidden in your interaction with another. The awareness skills — such as allowing space for listening, speaking with kindness, and expressing true feelings in a safe way — will help you cultivate new growth in your relationships. You will also explore the importance of creating rituals, which enhance your relationships with special and memorable moments.

Part 4, "One-Minute Mindfulness for Health and Well-Being," shows how bringing clarity and deep awareness to your self-care enhances your well-being. Health is essential for enjoying life in the next minute. This section shares several useful ways to calm the mind and to reduce anxiety, stress, negative thinking, and emotional eating. You will learn about an ancient practice, found in many traditions, that offers an affirming and direct way to sense and inhabit the body. The body is, after all, our container for contacting the next sixty seconds.

Part 5, "One-Minute Mindfulness for Nature, Spirituality, and Contemplation," touches the heart of what is nourishing and uplifting. By recapturing your childlike curiosity for all things natural and untamed, you can recharge and reinvigorate yourself in the very next moment. How often have you consciously attuned yourself to nature's rhythms or deepened your spiritual path with contemplation? This section demonstrates that no matter where you work or live, the riches of spirit and meaning can always be found with mindfulness.

For many, the journey of one-minute mindfulness will be like coming home to a comfortable and safe place. Living the next minute mindfully will connect some of you to hope and optimism. Others may find that focusing on the next sixty seconds initially brings anxiety, but eventually a deep sense of relief and peace, even in the midst of chaos, will replace the discomfort.

Awakening to this moment is an art, which you will express in a personal way. However you decide to shape your life as you sculpt your attention and awareness, it is my hope that *One-Minute Mindfulness* will give you powerful and fulfilling options to live your life one liberating minute at a time.

Part 1

One-Minute Mindfulness for

HOME AND PLAY

Engaging in one-minute mindfulness at home maximizes its nurturing potential in the place we count on for peace and rejuvenation. Play expands the heart, which cannot help but invite joy and wonder to join in the process. With every minute that you apply these approaches, you open yourself to a rich array of elevating and inspiring experiences.

Morning Awakens

Morning is untamed. The body is not quite ready; the mind is half dreaming. This is all the more reason to greet the day gently and with utmost care.

What do you do in the first sixty seconds of your morning? Is your mind filled with thoughts and worries about the day ahead? Do you drag your body out of bed like a heavy sack of potatoes? How can you bring yourself into the next sixty seconds with awareness and presence?

There's also the question of how you awaken. Does a buzzing alarm rattle you awake? Do you hit the snooze button several times because your body wants more sleep?

When you wake up and are still lying in bed, spend one minute noticing the body, from the toes up through the torso, arms, and neck to the head. Stay with your body for now; your mind will have enough time for thinking throughout the rest of the day. Do you notice bodily tension anywhere? As you do this, notice your breath and let it become smooth. Your breath is your intimate kiss with this moment.

Spend another sixty seconds listening to the music of the

morning. What do your room and the surrounding environment sound like in the morning? Let all the little creaks and crackles, the rustle of the sheets, the birds outside, the animals inside, maybe the movement and even the snores of a partner greet you while your head still rests upon its pillow.

We can learn a lot from watching a dog or a cat awaken. My own cat awakens slowly each morning. When he's ready, he stretches his gray, furry paws far in front of him and gracefully arches his back. It is a kitty yoga pose that he holds for up to five seconds, then repeats two or three more times within the first five minutes of getting up. He is, I figure, greeting the morning. What does your body's morning greeting look like? Be sure to include a long, peaceful stretch that prepares your body for a day of gravity-defying feats.

Be at peace with your body in this minute. Don't berate it, harangue it, or push it around. Ask for its help in this next minute as you rise and begin to move about; it will be serving as your helpful companion throughout the day.

As you stand, walk, and move about your space, listen to the morning's soft sounds. The morning light also offers effects that will not be duplicated later. If it's dim, notice the shade that the soft morning light offers. If it's dark, when you turn on a light, feel the light switch between your fingers. Notice your eyes adjusting to the light.

Pay attention to how many unique experiences there are in every minute, and see if you can notice even the slightest gratitude or appreciation for some or all of these happenings. Even if your morning time at home seems rushed, it actually offers a vast and open space. Give yourself permission to take it all in, for this is a morning like no other.

Today, give the gift of this unique morning to yourself.

PRACTICE

Slow down this morning. When you walk, know that you are walking. Feel the floor beneath your feet; sense each little movement. When you shower, know that you are showering. Listen intently to the running water. Note its temperature as it cascades over your skin. This morning, experience what it is like to let nothing go unfelt, unheard, or unnoticed.

Beckoning the Body

*T*he body knows things the thinking mind can only imagine. Its innate wisdom wants to be heard and shared with you in the next sixty seconds. And yet, rather than beckoning to it with care, sensitivity, and love, we find it easy to feel conflicted about the body.

One of two ways we get conflicted about the body is to grasp at it. For example, we can hold on too tightly to how it looks. This could well be because the body represents youth, strength, and beauty. But when we are overly concerned about staying young and mentally grasp at the body in this way, we get worried and anxious. Focusing on the body's external appearance is an attachment that can make us greedy to the point of desiring another body, like the one we saw on TV or at the fitness center. Comparing our body to another's can lead to dissatisfaction and unhappiness in the next minute. Has this ever happened to you?

The other way we get conflicted about the body is to reject it. We might reject it because we deem our body plain, not beautiful enough, or increasingly wrinkled, feeble, and old. This judgment can leave us feeling unhappy, fearful, frustrated, angry, bitter, and distraught every sixty seconds we spend looking at a mirror — and well beyond the time spent in front of it. Of course, we can try to fool ourselves with a lot of plastic surgery, but the body keeps aging in spite of any attempts to alter nature's course. Both of these approaches, grasping at or rejecting the body, are a recipe for pain and suffering.

One-minute mindfulness offers a more gentle and hospitable alternative. It begins with the question, What would it be like to fully and completely accept the body I have right now, for one entire minute, recognizing both its strengths and its weaknesses?

The body is no different from spectacular castles and monuments that also must eventually lose their luster. Aging and wrinkles are simply signs that we have lived in the castle. They do not diminish the purpose, wonder, and loveliness of the body that carries our spirit and manifests our deeds. Regardless of the body's external form, we can take to heart the sentiment poet and philosopher John O'Donohue shares in his book *Beauty*: "The world of the senses is intensified with beauty that is meant to recall us to the higher and eternal forms of beauty."[1]

Morning is an ideal time to remind yourself that the body is a gateway to the senses and a connection with exquisite forms of beauty both transient and eternal. When you wake in the morning, set aside the negative filters of thoughts, opinions, and perceptions that get between you and your body. Imagine instead seeing yourself through the eyes of someone who sees not your small external self but the eternal beauty that is present in you in every moment. At the start of the day, take a minute to let yourself settle into this spacious view of your true self. Notice what it's like to do this. Even if the filters are hard to remove, this practice enables you to identify them, which is the first step in removing them.

Loving and appreciating our own body takes time. One

helpful means of appreciating our own form is to consider the form of someone we love or admire. We might find this form in a photograph or in the cat, dog, or other animal we love. Take one minute during the day to study and appreciate the form of another living being, whether mammal, fish, insect, plant, or other. Though each of these has a form different from yours, each has its singular beauty, elegance, functionality, and grace.

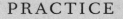

PRACTICE

Throughout the day, beckon your body simply by noticing your breath. Right now, or during any sixty seconds, notice how the breath comes into the body and how it leaves. For one minute, notice the breath. Whether the breath is slow, fast, long, or short, just be aware of it. Let yourself know the breath a little more intimately than you did sixty seconds ago. Let one minute of conscious breathing show you how beautiful it is to let go — one of the sublime teachings the breath offers.

First Taste, Last Taste

Without taste there would be much less temptation in the world. Taste is no small thing, and many wisdom stories tell us about the lasting consequences of wanting a little taste of something. We can honor and savor the power of taste by paying much greater attention to it.

Let's begin by taking a brief inventory of taste. Spend a few moments reflecting on your answer to the following question: What was the first thing you tasted this morning? Try to recall all you can about its flavor.

If your first thought was a food or a beverage, did you overlook previous tastes? Maybe the minty toothpaste that cleansed and awakened the ten thousand taste buds on your tongue and the roof of your mouth? Before that, did you taste the flavor of "morning mouth," when you opened your eyes and the alarm clock rang or the morning light streamed through the windows?

Taste is always with us, ever present. Even when you detect none, there is a flavor in the noneating mouth. One-minute mindfulness can help you savor that cereal, egg, yogurt, bread, tea, coffee, or other food you feed your body in the morning as well as throughout the day. Some people are so rushed in the morning that they skip breakfast because it takes time — although breakfast may be one of the most important sixty-second choices we make at the start of our day. Others quickly gobble up breakfast, as though eating were an unwanted chore.

The first time I met with a client I'll call Kevin, he shared a story of being frustrated, irritable, and quick to anger with his family. When I asked for his theory on why this was happening, Kevin said the problem was a result of financial stress. After more questioning, I discovered that he didn't practice good self-care. Kevin rarely started a day with any protein, compensating instead with a significant jolt of caffeine to get himself going.

I explained to Kevin how his nutritional choices were affecting his thinking, how the brain's frontal cortex, where judging, analyzing, and decision making occur, needs protein every two or three hours. For the next week, Kevin made a one-minute mindfulness choice to eat a peanut butter and jelly sandwich in the morning and to cut his caffeine intake by half. To his surprise, his irritability soon disappeared, his family was happier, and he was better prepared to deal with his financial struggles.

You can make your first taste of the day count too. When it's time, take sixty seconds to fully commit to what you are about to do. Eating is one of our most intimate acts. Pause to consider that the morsel you choose to put into your mouth is about to merge with you — you can't get much more intimate than that! The right food will nourish and build cells and sustain you with energy. Slowing down to taste and chew your food actually helps the enzymes in your mouth's saliva start the process of digesting carbohydrates and fats. In the next sixty seconds, you can also reflect on the intricate web of natural resources and people that brought this first taste to you.

When you engage in a mindful minute of tasting that first bite or sip, instead of a throwaway moment, you have manifested a morning's first taste that is distinctly memorable. At the end of the day, you will still have that first taste to remember. How many times could you say this was so in the past?

PRACTICE

Just as you can make the first taste of the day count, the last taste of the day can be special too. The last taste is an opportunity to acknowledge your fullness and satisfaction. It can signify finding balance. Don't take the last taste for granted. End your day by eating consciously and skillfully. What do you want your last taste of the day to be? A soothing cup of aromatic tea? A glass of chilled water?

By paying attention to your first and last tastes, you are on the road to making more mindful food choices throughout the day and to cultivating a nurturing attitude toward yourself. You might want to create a "first taste–last taste journal." Who knows what insights you'll find?

4. Nurturing the Moment

*D*o your days often feel like a blur? Are you just trying hard to keep up with the avalanche of activities before you — paying the bills, answering a growing stack of emails, picking up and dropping off the kids, and meeting constant deadlines in all their forms? You know it's time to slow down the busy mind if you're asking yourself, *Do moments of calm really exist?* The good news is that you have the power, in the very next minute, to reverse the overstimulation, excessive activity, constant planning, and anxiety that keep your brain in overdrive.

When I was in the monastery, I learned a simple technique from an elder monk. He gave me a rosary made of 108 beads and told me to close my eyes and count one bead for every breath I took until I reached the end of the rosary. It sounded easy to me at the time, but it wasn't. This practice builds attention and focus and sharpens an ability to increasingly notice, and appreciate, how those little moments offer kernels of peace, joy, and rejuvenation.

Try it yourself, and see if you don't still accomplish your goals but with more presence and enjoyment. Instead of a rosary, you can use each breath as a bead. In the next minute, count each breath you take. It might help to close your eyes. Most people take from eight to ten breaths a minute. If you lose count, don't worry; just begin again. Try this now.

What was that like for you? If you noticed a crowd of thoughts between your counts, that's okay. Taking one minute to connect with your breath and to focus your attention has an impact nonetheless. I recommend you practice this technique any time you feel frazzled, anxious, and weary from overthinking or worrying. In time, regularly practicing this technique will leave you feeling noticeably refreshed and focused.

What does nurturing mean for you? Nurturing can be expressed and found in many different ways. For example, take a minute now to look around your surroundings and find something that is pleasing or nourishing — a favorite color, texture, sound, object, or shape. Don't limit your options. Look outside too, in the backyard, on the street, through a window.

Another way to nourish ourselves is to set healthy boundaries, which includes limiting the time we spend watching TV and using technology. An easy way to learn whether you need to change your habits is to notice the times when you feel bored, drained, sad, upset, or constricted. It could be that you simply need to change something in your environment. For example, if a news program is making you anxious or upset, take action in the next sixty seconds and change the channel or turn off the TV.

Whenever you notice you are doing something that is not truly satisfying, make the sixty-second decision to turn to a more nurturing and fulfilling activity. A wonderful thing about being human is that focusing the mind on what is nurturing right now simultaneously turns it away from whatever brings discomfort. Isn't it empowering to know that how you decide to use the next minute is wholly up to you?

PRACTICE

Choose one unsatisfying habit you would like to change because you recognize that it does not represent the person you see yourself to be. The habit could be anything, such as smoking, emotional eating, opinionated behavior, or procrastination. Next, write down several nurturing activities you could substitute for the old habit, and make sure that these activities can be initiated in a minute, such as reading a book, taking a short walk, stretching, calling a friend, listening to uplifting music, or taking a few meditative breaths. Finally, rehearse this in detail mentally; see yourself stopping the old habit and turning to the new activity. Practice this visualization until the new behavior feels natural. Stay with the new activity for several minutes. After visualizing the change, you are ready to make the change in real time. It takes one minute to begin. Congratulations on taking these steps to nurture yourself!

5. Stepping over the Threshold

*T*hresholds await us at every turn. They are important transition points. They are those defining moments when intention crystallizes into choice, leading us away from the past and into the unfolding sixty seconds. Each doorway we pass through, figuratively or literally, transports us to the next situation in which to be present and authentic. How will you make the next threshold count?

Have you ever counted the number of thresholds you pass through on a typical day? They can be experienced as a movement in physical space — through a literal doorway or entryway — but also as thresholds of time (as with deadlines and schedules), emotion (moving into and out of feeling states), and energy (levels of hunger, tiredness, and vitality, for example). Whatever form a threshold takes, it can be a reminder to set an intention for each minute of the transition. Buddha spoke of this when he said:

It is unwise to do things that bring regret
And require repentance,

To cause suffering for oneself
And a weeping and tearful face.

It is wise to do things which do not require repentance
But bring joy and fulfillment,
Happiness and delight.[2]

I find it useful to set an intention when walking from one room to another. This only takes a few seconds and allows me to focus on the purpose of each move; in a broader sense, it gives direction to my day. Often, I like to take a moment of silence, pause with a breath, and then mentally say the following words:

In the next minute,
may I be open to each moment.
May my actions be kind,
May they be beneficial,
May they be of service.

Intentions like this help us to center and to relieve the anxiety that transition often produces. You can use the intention above, but it also helps to set intentions for different times of the day so as to stay connected to your purpose. You can create a morning intention, an afternoon intention, and an evening intention. Tailor each to what you are doing at that time of day. Here's an example:

This morning/afternoon/evening,
as I go about my daily tasks,
above all else, may I be
sensitive, kind, and compassionate
to the needs of myself and others.

PRACTICE

Learn more about your personal thresholds by creating a "threshold journal" to help you identify the different transitions you face daily. Try dividing a page into four columns: Physical Thresholds, Time Thresholds, Emotional Thresholds, and Energy Thresholds. For the difficult thresholds, write a specific sixty-second intention that can help you transition. Get in the practice of using these intentions throughout the day.

Below is another intention I like to use, based on the 2,500-year-old Buddhist loving-kindness practice:

May I be safe,
May I be happy,
May I be healthy,
May I be peaceful.

Reorganize Your Routines

*R*outines and schedules are intended to give structure. Like maps, they provide a plan for reaching a goal. Routines work best when they serve as containers for our energy and one-minute awareness. But sometimes they become useless, outmoded, and inappropriate for what is really happening in the moment. Has a routine ever become so much a part of you that you accepted it without further question?

Jeremy, a fellow in his forties who worked for a city fire department, suffered from an inflexible routine. In our first meeting, he described the weekly inspections and the standard of cleanliness the firehouse enforced with almost military strictness. Jeremy also described how each day after returning home from work, instead of greeting his family, he headed straight for the kitchen to do an inspection. If there were any dishes in the sink, he immediately started washing them — and fuming at the same time. As you might imagine, this didn't sit well with his wife and children, and before long there was a revolt. To his credit, Jeremy worked hard to let go of fixed inappropriate routines. Approaching his time at home in one-minute increments, he learned to be more flexible.

What are some of your fixed behaviors and routines at home? For example, consider where you eat your meals and what you do during mealtime or the order in which you shower, brush your teeth, get dressed, and eat breakfast. What are your priorities on weekends? What would it be like for you to re-arrange some of your routines? (Of course, I'm not suggesting you dress first and shower afterward!) Give some thought to the consequences of one or more of your routines. If, for example, you spend hours watching sports on TV, you may be missing out on meaningful opportunities with others. Drinking regularly can also be a mindless routine that saps the energy out of relation-ships and numbs us to the next sixty seconds of our lives.

It takes courage to change routines, even minor ones, but more fully living each moment is what's at stake. Even if a rou-tine is useful, that doesn't mean it has to be mind-numbing. Enter each routine today with the intention and freedom to experience it directly, consciously — without falling into habit or letting your mind travel elsewhere while your body moves automati-cally. For example, do you know what color socks you are wear-ing at this moment? What color are the buttons on your blouse or shirt? Is there anything unique about the stitching or fabric?

Lots of unexpected — and sometimes unfortunate — things can happen when we get robotic. I have a good friend who told me that he got dressed one morning, made his coffee, got into his car, and headed to work. He had traveled several miles when he noticed his legs were cold. He glanced down and discovered that he had forgotten to put on his pants! Now there was a wake-up call to be more present — fortunately, not a disastrous one.

If we're not careful, routines can rob us of the experience of the next minute. Be watchful and enter your routines with moment-to-moment awareness. When we vary any routine, we refresh our experience. The following practice will help you think about the emotions that may be holding established routines in place.

PRACTICE

I call this practice, which I often use in workshops, "What Does It Mean to Reorganize My Surroundings?" It's more than an investigation of our routines; it's a look at how we can learn to embrace the process of changing a routine.

To begin, write down your answers to the following questions about rearranging your surroundings:

- *How could I create a more comfortable space in the next sixty seconds?*
- *How would others feel about moving furniture and other things around?*
- *What concerns, worries, or even fears do I have about changing things around?*
- *What would it be like to rearrange things just for the sake of rearranging them?*
- *What pieces would I move first?*
- *What items would be most difficult to move, both physically and emotionally?*
- *Do I need new furniture to effectively rearrange things?*
- *How long would the process take? How long could I allow it to take?*
- *What are the potential advantages of reorganizing?*
- *What are the potential disadvantages?*
- *What expectations or demands do I place on reorganizing?*
- *What is the worst thing that could happen if I reorganized?*

Live with I-Thou Kindness

A t times, kindness can seem almost inconceivable, as fragile and unlikely as a snowflake in the middle of a triple-digit heat wave. Yet despite the harshness and demands of life, kindness persists. A slow and determined message of hope riding along a superhighway of reactivity and emotion, each small kindness given or received is evidence that life is worthwhile.

When we harness the next minute with kindness, we do what is decent and fundamentally good. As Buddhist meditation teacher Sharon Salzberg writes, "We do good because it frees the heart. It opens us to a wellspring of happiness. We can begin to view our aspirations in this light. We aspire to good in order to grow, to yield, to become more and more open, more connected, to be happy ourselves, and thus happy for others."[3] Kindness is not a trivial, perfunctory, or obligatory action; it is the deepest recognition that we're all in this together — doing the best we can in the friendship, family, neighborhood, city, nation, planet that we cohabit.

On occasion most of us have turned away from others in our lives, even in subtle ways. You know you are turning away if you are distracted, not paying attention, too busy, lost in your habits, reactive, angry, or just stuck in your own thoughts. Fortunately, kindness offers an infinite number of ways to exercise our freedom to respond, to turn toward our family, friends, and others. Through kindness, we access what the twentieth-century philosopher Martin Buber termed "the I-Thou relationship," a perspective from which we enter into a dynamic, living relationship with another. The I-Thou relationship is the alternative to the "I-It relationship."[4]

Try this one-minute experiment of shifting into I-Thou kindness with the next person you come into contact with. It requires that you be fully open, engaged, playful, and empathetic with another while expecting nothing in return. You might express anything from a simple smile to interest in another's hobbies or concerns. I-Thou kindness also means being happy for someone else's happiness or path, even if you don't agree with that path — a path, of course, that does not cause harm to others. Notice what you find pleasing in others, such as their clothing or the color of their eyes, and let them know the moment you notice. Why wait?

Another aspect of kindness is recognizing and managing negative emotions. When we can't be kind, at least we can refrain from harming others in the next minute. Although more passive, this is still a form of heart-centered, I-Thou kindness. It honors the intention not to harm another. Do factor in that it's not easy to avoid emotional reactivity throughout an entire lifetime — some of it is a style of thinking we learned, perhaps from our family of origin, and some of it is due to the brain's negativity bias. According to neuropsychologist Rick Hanson, "Your brain is like Velcro for negative experiences and Teflon for positive ones — even though most of your experiences are probably neutral or positive.

…and in relationships, it typically takes about five positive interactions to overcome the effects of a single negative one."[5]

Don't let this discourage you, though. Our brains are amazingly and wonderfully flexible and adaptable. Each time you express a kindness you are rewiring your brain. To "prime the pump," it helps to recall a kindness you've experienced in your own life. In the next sixty seconds, reflect on a kindness someone showed you that really made a difference. This could be something you remember from childhood, adolescence, or a more recent experience. Take your time and immerse yourself in the positive feeling of this kindness. If you have difficulty, imagine anything that has made you feel good, even the kindness of a beloved pet.

If practicing kindness comes easily for you, enjoy and spread the joy. If this is new work for you, start with little kindnesses, wherever you may find them in the next minute.

PRACTICE

Today, keep in mind the following important question: What is one small kindness I can offer in the next sixty seconds? Whenever the question arises in your mind, go into action. Send a kind email, smile at the next person you meet, or give someone a genuine compliment. If you don't interact with anyone today, extend a kindness to yourself, whether an affirmation or self-acknowledgment. Don't waste any potential sixty-second kindness.

Playtime for the Soul

*O*riginally adapted from Dutch, the old English word *plegian* signified physical actions such as exercising and frolicking. Today, the meaning of the verb *to play* has expanded the scope of that original definition. Yet in our work-obsessed culture, the idea of taking time to play can have negative connotations. Have you ever had the thought or feeling that when you are playing, you are not being productive or useful?

Play and work are not meant to be pitted against each other. Play is how we rejoice and how we can live life in the next sixty seconds, whether or not we're working. One-minute mindfulness can help to dissolve the distinction between work and play while encouraging us to experience both simultaneously.

Some meditation and retreat centers ask those attending a retreat to accept work assignments. This means that doctors, university professors, and bankers might be scrubbing bathroom floors and toilets during a retreat. Take the next minute to consider how you would respond to the task of getting on your knees to meticulously clean and polish a porcelain public commode. How do you perform this task at home? While thinking about this, do you notice any resistance? Did you think about the smell and scrunch up your face in disgust at the thought of this task? I'm not saying that there's anything wrong with scrubbing a toilet, and I'm not saying that you should make it your life's goal. I am saying that the resistance we bring to any task makes it difficult. Scrubbing is just scrubbing, odor is just odor, and kneeling is just kneeling. The alternatives to resistance are acceptance and willingness. Are you willing to experience the chores you do in your household as something new?

In her late thirties, Roxanne, a mother of three young children, came into my office frowning one day. I soon learned that she was utterly exhausted from caring for her children and their home. She was so overwhelmed with trying to make things perfect that she found it almost impossible to make the simplest decisions. When Roxanne's partner, Barry, joined us in a session, he sadly shared: "She's not the 'silly girl' I fell in love with, someone who knew how to have fun. Now she's this 'serious girl' who sees life as a burden, and I feel judged for not trying hard enough because I have a lighter approach to life." Roxanne was somewhat shocked to hear this, but she made a commitment right then to embrace a more playful attitude — this included accepting a more lived-in, imperfect house.

You don't have to travel to Las Vegas, take a cruise to Mexico, or go anywhere to play and lighten up. If there is an old script running in your head about needing to take things seriously or be productive all the time, use the next sixty seconds to find a more joyful and less restrictive view. In fact, for anyone who is depressed, lonely, or in pain, playtime is a powerful antidote and a valuable gift. Even if no one is around, find an alternative to being serious. Watch a funny movie and laugh for no good reason.

PRACTICE

Even when there are stresses and chores and schedules to maintain, experiment with a playful attitude. See how it can transform the next minute of your day. If you find it difficult to be playful, spend some time watching children play or remembering how you played when you were young. If it helps, write down some playful activities you can begin to reconnect with. Remember that you don't have to recreate the wheel. Use what worked for you in the past in order to find the silly, jolly person within.

Skipping is a childlike activity you can try in the next sixty seconds — of course, take care not to hurt yourself. I know of an office where the staff read the chapter "Do One Joyful Thing Right Now" in my book The Mindfulness Code *and then decided to enjoy skipping together for an afternoon.[6] They sure did laugh a lot!*

9. Gratitude for the Day

Gratitude is not a magic trick, yet it can make a half-empty glass appear half full. It can transform difficult moments because it has a way of making the littlest things more significant and meaningful. Gratitude can even transform what previously filled us with envy and jealousy.

Scientists have begun to measure the effects of gratitude. For example, researchers from the University of California at Davis and the University of Miami assigned participants in three related gratitude studies to one of three different groups. The first group was instructed to pay attention to and keep track of daily hassles, annoyances, and irritants. The second group was instructed to notice experiences of gratitude as they were happening and to make a list of these. The third group was the control group; this group noted neutral life events. All participants also tracked their moods, time spent sleeping, and time spent exercising. The study found that those who paid attention to experiences of gratitude were 25 percent happier than those who paid attention to daily annoyances. The gratitude group also reported more optimism and spent more time exercising than the other two groups. The researchers concluded, "The effect on positive affect appeared to be the most robust finding. Results suggest that a conscious focus on blessings may have emotional and interpersonal benefits."[7] No wonder the practice of gratitude is an effective clinical intervention for depression.

What forms of gratitude have touched you today? Yesterday? This past week? If none come to mind, don't be hard on yourself. Even the most beautiful view can be taken for granted when you see it every day, just as the blessing of good health commonly goes unappreciated.

In Zen Buddhism, there is a term for overcoming the tendency to overlook all the graces that surround us. It is "beginner's mind" or "don't-know mind," and it's a reminder to constantly let go of all our preconceived ideas. Beginner's mind asks us to contact and experience whatever is happening as if for the first time — be it a sunset or greeting our loved ones when they come home at the end of the day. Don't-know mind opens us to the possibility that the next sixty seconds will unfold with their own beauty and wonder. This is an exciting way to approach life, because as Zen master Shunryu Suzuki writes, "In the beginner's mind there are many possibilities, but in the expert's there are few."[8]

Locating gratitude is a way to cope with life's difficult, stressful, and negative experiences. Gratitude is not only what we feel inwardly but also what we express toward others. In this way, we strengthen the bonds of our relationships. Try making a moment of gratitude part of a mealtime blessing. This can give the entire family an opportunity to express thankfulness while learning more about one another's daily experiences.

Gratitude is a potent vaccine that inoculates us against negativity. If you are feeling any kind of negative emotion, you can counteract it in the next sixty seconds by noticing something for which you're grateful. Use the next minute to ask others what they are grateful for. Gratitude is a means of overcoming short-term pleasure seeking. It lets us tap into deeper and more sustainable ways of experiencing fulfillment. Besides, when we're grateful for what we already have, we don't have a reason to be disappointed.

PRACTICE

Here is a gratitude practice that can have an immediate impact on your life. Every three or four days, look back over that time period and write down three to five things that happened at home for which you are grateful. This could be appreciation for a kind act someone did for you or for any of the little things in your life — that comfortable chair, the flavor of a particular food, the book you are reading, the music you love, the hot water in your shower. (You are not limited to five items.) Do this for a four-week period to see how it affects your life. You might even track how gratitude impacts your mood, your sleep, how you eat, exercise, and interact with others.

10. Sacred Nighttime

*N*ighttime invites a tempo all its own. As darkness falls, an ancient circadian rhythm all primates share signals us to become tired. At around 7:00 PM, our bodies begin to secrete melatonin to induce sleepiness. By 8:30 PM, the digestive system is suppressed. This is how it has always been for all our ancestors. A day of busyness is followed with a sacred antidote, designed to refresh the body, enliven the mind, replenish the spirit, and consolidate the day's learning.

In the modern world, all that has changed with daylight savings time, electricity, working across time zones, late-night TV, computers, cell phones, and other inventions that delay the production of sleep-inducing melatonin to alter our built-in biological cycle. How can nighttime's purpose be honored when it is forced to compete with an increase of 24/7 forms of stimulation and reward, from video games to social networking websites?

If you doubt that sleep is a treasure that needs to be protected, consider this: it takes only three days of reduced sleep to put the body into a chronic stress state, which can create daytime cognitive issues and suppress the immune system. Research has shown that lack of sleep can severely impact other areas of our lives as well, such as our appetites, which often leads to obesity. One study showed that individuals who slept more than eight hours a night weighed significantly less than those who slept only five hours a night. According to this study, stress caused by lack of sleep stimulated the hormone ghrelin, which increases hunger, while decreasing the hormone leptin, which suppresses the appetite.[9]

Do you respect your body's ancient biological rhythms? You can begin to foster an island of quiet nurturing in preparation for sleep in a minute's time. If you live with others, share what you've learned with them. Consider winding down slowly each night by saying goodnight to your electronic helpers; the light from electronic devices delays sleep by about an hour. Creating a healthy boundary around technology is an important part of respecting your body, brain, and spirit. Do you answer your phone even after you have gone to bed? Some of the young people I've worked with answer text messages in the middle of the night! I'm not suggesting that you go off the grid, but do recognize the daytime benefits that come from a little nighttime nurturing.

It takes only your awareness in the minutes before bedtime to develop a ritual that will make your sleep more satisfying. I recall a recent winter when the power went out in my neighborhood for four days. Fortunately, I had a wood-burning stove for warmth and for heating up tea and canned foods. Without the distraction of TV and other devices, I became more aware of my body's rhythms. Since it was January, I got sleepy shortly after the sun went down. After getting a good fire going, reading by candlelight for a while, and enjoying some hot tea, I was bundled up and ready to sleep before 7:30 PM. (I knew the time because my wristwatch still worked.)

PRACTICE

Create a sleep ritual that balances your need for evening activity and a good night's rest. Use the next sixty seconds to write down some steps that will encourage better sleep. These might include eyeshades or curtains that block outside light; slow, gentle stretching; a cup of chamomile tea or milk; and soothing music or reading to help quiet your mind and muscles. (Vigorous exercise within an hour of sleep is stimulating and will keep you up.) Be patient as you find a new way to relate to nighttime.

Part 2

One-Minute Mindfulness for

WORK AND CREATIVITY

One-minute mindfulness at work can fundamentally transform your experience of daily tasks. It can help you tap into a deeper sense of purpose and turn on the lamp of creativity. It also offers you, in the next minute, the opportunity to get out of your head and reconnect to your body in a profound way.

11. Driving as Preparation

*T*he act of driving requires our full attention. I know of a woman who drove through her garage door one morning because she was on automatic pilot and didn't notice that it was still closed! The lapse of a split second can have devastating results. How do you approach your morning drive?

Do you use the morning drive to prepare for the day to come? Is driving a placeholder, a time for fitting in extraneous activities? Do you let the frustrations of the road soak into your body and spirit, filling you with anger or draining you of energy? A one-minute mindfulness approach to driving can improve your emotional tone, stress level, and ability to be open and adaptable.

When I discuss the brain and multitasking in workshops, I often ask participants to share stories about multitasking while driving. Here are a few that stand out: eating soup, with a spoon; putting on makeup and getting dressed; reading the newspaper or a book, even on a busy freeway; simultaneously smoking a cigarette, drinking a cup of coffee, putting on mascara, and backing up the car.

Ample evidence shows that the brain does not multitask

very well. A recent study showed that simply talking while driving can negatively impact our driving skills. Researchers also found the reverse to be true: driving reduces a driver's ability to recall a conversation by as much as 20 percent.[10] According to psycholinguist Gary Dell, one of the study's researchers, "You might think that talking is an easy thing to do and that comprehending language is easy. But it's not. Speech production and speech comprehension are attention-demanding activities, and so they...compete with other tasks that require your attention — like driving."[11] In other words, something will suffer if we decide to split our attention when we're behind the wheel.

Basically, there are two ways to drive. The first is to drive in order to get where we're going. Driving then is a means to an end, an act that has little intrinsic value. In this case, we may be preoccupied with other things when we get in the car. Our minds may wander off to the future. Maybe we're engaged in a conversation with someone, literally or mentally, as we pull into the street. Our attention might be focused on listening to a radio station or thoughts about an upcoming task. I'm not suggesting that we avoid all sources of sensory input while driving but that we practice sixty-second intervals of awareness to notice when we are driving mindlessly, with our bodies going through the motions.

Fortunately, there's a second way to go about this: drive with the sole purpose of driving. It's that simple and direct. It's about full participation in what we are doing with the next sixty seconds, before we even climb into the car and turn on the ignition. For example, what details do you notice about your vehicle's door handle as you open the door? Its temperature, shape, the feel of it? How does your body bend and move as you climb into the driver's seat? Feel your hands as they grip the steering wheel.

Notice the sound of the pavement as the tires move along the road's surface.

When we bring awareness to the next minute, we gain traction instead of dis-traction with our surroundings, from road signs and road conditions to bicyclists and pedestrians. We can also find gratitude each time we drive somewhere. Fully participating in the journey of moving from one place to another leaves no time for anxiety about the future. Driving in order to drive requires our presence in each moment — and that sets our consciousness to sixty-second time.

PRACTICE

In the next day or week, take one driving trip where you are focused only on your driving, with no distractions. Do this when you are alone, and try to be as present as you can every sixty seconds. You don't have to be perfect when doing this. When your mind wanders, to the past or the future, gently bring it back. You can even mentally affirm your present moment intention with the words "driving, driving."

12. Walk with Dignity and Grace

Where we walk, there moves our lives. Each step is the culmination of direction, coordination, and balance. As commonplace as walking is, each stride we take is our unique signature. Walking teaches us to slow down and to inhabit each unfolding minute. When we do, we're not at risk of losing the pleasure philosopher Søren Kierkegaard describes: "Most men pursue pleasure with such breathless haste that they hurry past it."[12]

Walking reveals many fascinating lessons, including an understanding of how to move through the world. Do you walk quickly and heavily, focused on your needs, with little care for what you disturb along the way? Or do you tread lightly and carefully, with awareness of others and your environment as you navigate your needs and desires? Perhaps the truth to be found in walking is this: the opportunity to walk without grasping for anything else, and thereby touch peace and contentment. We can fully embrace each step, craving nothing else, knowing the world has nothing more precious to offer than right now. With each step, we learn to walk our own uneven path — how liberating!

You can begin a purifying and healing walk in the next sixty seconds. Don't be surprised if this exercise of taking each step mindfully affects your balance; you can always use a nearby wall for stability. To let go of all craving in your next step, embrace beginner's mind and release expectations. For now, take your normal walking program off autopilot. As you lift your foot, know that you are lifting your foot. Place your awareness in the foot as you observe which part of it rises up first and which part is the last to lift upward. Notice the lightness, the airy quality in lifting. Slow down as you lift your foot so that you can feel even how your clothes move across your leg. As you move your foot and leg forward, be fully aware that they are moving forward. Appreciate how the knee bends and how the hip moves as the foot deliberately and slowly moves through space.

As you set your foot down, know that you are setting it down. Be aware of how quickly or slowly it moves toward the ground. If there is anticipation of the foot touching the ground, observe the anticipation. Feel how gravity moves the leg downward and how the foot finds support from the earth when it lands. Contact the ground fully, feeling how the heel touches first and how other parts of the foot then make contact.

As your weight shifts when your foot settles down, know that the weight is shifting. Feel the strength and support in the leg now bearing weight. Find that one instant when you are equally balanced between the left and the right legs. As you continue walking mindfully, notice how each step and each surface is dynamic, how it changes. If you are wearing shoes, notice how your foot moves in the shoe and how the shoe lifts and later makes contact with the ground. With each step, know that nothing needs to be different, added, or subtracted. There is just this body taking this one step — then another step and then the next. When you turn, know that you are turning and changing direction. Remember too to take time to pay attention to your surroundings. Don't miss out on the view!

After spending a minute walking in this way, reflect on what it would be like to extend this level of intentionality, deliberateness, grace, and composure to other movements in your life.

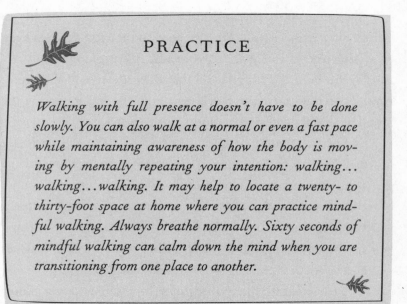

PRACTICE

Walking with full presence doesn't have to be done slowly. You can also walk at a normal or even a fast pace while maintaining awareness of how the body is moving by mentally repeating your intention: walking... walking...walking. It may help to locate a twenty- to thirty-foot space at home where you can practice mindful walking. Always breathe normally. Sixty seconds of mindful walking can calm down the mind when you are transitioning from one place to another.

13. Finding Purpose

*P*urpose is never far away. You can perform your work while feeling numb, resentful, or bitter, merely getting through your day, but with the light of purpose, you can find meaning in your work, an opportunity for learning and service and even adventure. Is it the job that unlocks a door to meaning, or do you hold the key to freedom, doing the work you already do? Like the sun, purpose can brighten and warm your experience of each new minute.

Walter Russell, an early-twentieth-century writer and painter, never graduated from high school, yet he planned and built several buildings in New York. He was also a scientist and a sculptor. He created the Mark Twain Memorial and carved statues of Franklin Roosevelt and Thomas Edison, among others. Russell believed that purpose and inspiration were vital to any kind of achievement. He wrote, "You must love anything you must do. Do it not only cheerfully but lovingly and the very best way you know how."[13]

Love of work can be a difficult principle to grasp if your job is not fulfilling or you are focusing on what you get from a job instead of what you can give. This reminds me of William, a highly educated man in his thirties; he was depressed because he was unable to follow his chosen career path. The first few times William came to my office, he never smiled, and I wondered if the deep furrows in his face were permanently etched there. Bitter and miserable, he directed his frustration at the dismal economy and at his current job. He answered telephones eight hours a day. Any form of happiness in this job was not even remotely on William's map. But eventually, he began to see an alternate view he had been missing out on. He saw that his work did provide a meaningful service, and when William changed his attitude and brought more attention to his job, he got a promotion. Whether or not he moves on to a career he wants, William is consciously participating in his life. And isn't it better to have a purpose now instead of unhappily waiting for something better to come along?

Ultimately, the purpose we find must come from within. Don't take the easy way out by expecting a job to do all the heavy lifting. In the next sixty seconds, reflect on this question: How can I find inspiration in what I do? Now take a few more minutes to consider these questions as well: What helpful attitude can I bring to the people I meet through my work? Is there a challenging aspect to my work that can keep me engaged? How does my work serve others? How does it serve my life? What can I learn from this work that can broaden my perspective? How can I bring more vitality and joy to what I do?

Again, this inquiry does not mean resigning yourself to work you don't like or giving up on your dreams. By all means continue to pursue that special job or career that resonates with you. But while you do, choose not to drain yourself by resisting what is already in your life. Not having a special job in the short term doesn't mean you can't make a short-term job special. You bring to it what no one else offfers. Begin now, in the next sixty seconds.

PRACTICE

Whatever work you are currently involved in, make a list of all the ways that your job serves others. Someone who cleans the streets and sidewalks of leaves and debris, for example, serves by beautifying the out-of-doors, making the sidewalks safer to walk on, and bringing cause for pride into the community. There's also the opportunity to meet neighbors while performing such work. Find at least three ways that your work provides service to others, and each day, let this list guide you to connect with your purpose.

14. De-stress Your Inner Space

Stress is a killer — literally. Like a stealth fighter, stress hormones home in on the body's immune system and impair its ability to fight illness, while the hormone cortisol attacks neurons in the brain's learning center, the hippocampus. Some people think that stress pushes them to produce and to be more creative, but the truth is that chronic stress dumbs down the brain and leaves us vulnerable to sicknesses, making us less productive over time.

On a recent flight, I was talking with a couple when the conversation turned to the topic of stress. In a loud voice, the man proudly told me, "I don't like to hold in my stress. I find that if I yell and get angry at work, that gets it out of my system." "That's fine for you," his wife chimed in, "but what about the people around you?"

In the next minute, you can perform a stress-defying maneuver, and you can do it one breath at a time. Your stress doesn't have to spill onto others who happen to be in the line of fire. Working with the breath is an ancient and highly effective stress-management technique. It takes advantage of the body's natural wiring and lowers blood pressure and pulse and respiration rates. Also, by causing the abdominal cavity to press on the vagus nerve, a cranial nerve that connects the gut to the heart and the brain, the breath helps the gut release serotonin, the feel-good neurotransmitter, into the bloodstream.

When we breathe into the deepest part of the lungs, the diaphragm pushes down on the abdominal cavity and the abdomen expands, pushing out the stomach in front and pressing on the vagus nerve in back. This kind of controlled breathing is also known as diaphragmatic breathing and belly breathing. Only breathing high up in the chest leaves us vulnerable to the stress response. To locate the expanse of your breath, place one palm on your chest and the other on your stomach; then, while taking normal breaths, notice which palm is moving. If you're not sure, do this in front of a mirror. If you find movement in both hands or more movement in the hand on your chest, you need to move the breath lower. The idea is to take a normal breath and direct it into the deepest part of the lungs, in the same way that a few drops of water naturally flow to the bottom of a cup. Visualize your breath going into your abdomen as you take your next breath. Relax your belly and allow it to move freely. If you find that this is difficult, try gently clasping your hands behind your back. This will hinge your ribs open a bit, making it easier to take a fuller breath. If you get lightheaded, you may be taking too deep a breath. Don't give up on this. Simply try again.

When you find a deep, relaxed, and satisfying breath, practice it for one minute. How does it make you feel? Does it invite feelings of calm, clarity, warmth, and relaxation? You have just discovered a way to positively affect your body chemistry.

PRACTICE

Practice controlled diaphragmatic breathing for one minute at a time at least three times a day. Notice how it helps you cope, and how it refreshes your mind. In particular, use this breathing technique when you feel as though your mind is spinning and losing focus. Also notice your posture and how it may be affecting your ability to take a deep, diaphragmatic breath. Eventually, you can retrain yourself to enjoy the benefits of breathing like this whenever you need to.

Spread Optimism

Optimism is more than just a feel-good attitude. It is a life raft that staves off depression and feelings of helplessness every minute you apply it. Optimism is contagious. It deepens our connection with others, establishes new resources, and brings a sense of hope to all. Optimism strengthens our ability to bounce back from obstacles and acts like a magnet that draws others to us. It is a leadership quality, catalyzing widespread positive changes.

In his landmark book *Learned Optimism*, psychologist Martin Seligman draws upon extensive research to explain why optimism quickly quells feelings of depression and pessimism prolongs them, and the reasons make a lot of sense. Use the next minute to answer the following questions, and see if you have a tendency for pessimism.

- When something goes awry in your work life, do you usually assume it is your fault and that you could have done better?
- When something negative happens, do you look at the past and think that it's always been this way and that it's unlikely to change any time soon?

- Do you let problems at work affect your home life?
- When something bad happens, does it create despair about other areas of your life as well?

Answering yes to these questions indicates that you interpret negative events personally, view them as permanent, and allow them to color all areas of your life. Because pessimism feeds the belief that we will fail again, it's no wonder it makes us feel disheartened. It's like a stain you can't remove. Fortunately, optimistic thinking scrubs out tough stains with supportive explanations of challenging situations. According to Seligman, when we understand circumstances to be "temporary, specific, and external," it alleviates self-blame and allows for hope.[14]

When we experience disappointment or rejection, what matter most are the words or stories we tell ourselves. In the next sixty seconds, try out an optimistic thinking style by practicing the following statements. For maximum effect, say these out loud while looking in the mirror.

- There is no reason to blame myself because [fill in the blank] is happening right now. This is temporary. There is always a possibility for something better to occur.
- My whole life isn't destined to fall apart just because I'm experiencing challenges at work. I still have [fill in the blank], and I am grateful.
- I am a successful and effective person even though there are factors outside my control, such as [fill in the blank]. I am resilient, and I will persevere.

Thinking styles don't magically and instantly change. This week begin to notice whether you tend toward pessimism or optimism when dealing with difficult issues. Make it a new part of your daily routine to find an optimistic statement or affirmation you can share with another person the first minute you arrive at work or school. Share an uplifting story that either has happened to you or you have heard. Make sure you always include the important detail of how this story makes you feel. When you spread good news and optimism, you lend hope to others. When people hear that you feel happy, hopeful, resilient, resolute, and enthusiastic, they get tuned in to the same optimistic frequency and find it in their own lives too.

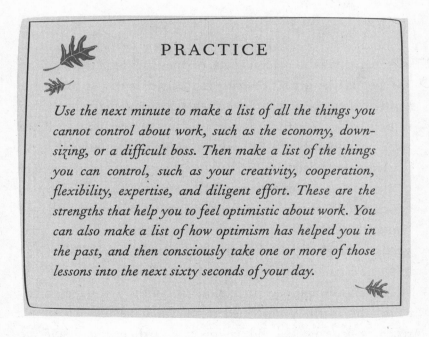

PRACTICE

Use the next minute to make a list of all the things you cannot control about work, such as the economy, downsizing, or a difficult boss. Then make a list of the things you can control, such as your creativity, cooperation, flexibility, expertise, and diligent effort. These are the strengths that help you to feel optimistic about work. You can also make a list of how optimism has helped you in the past, and then consciously take one or more of those lessons into the next sixty seconds of your day.

16. Unleash Creativity

*C*reativity is a natural state of mind. With creativity, no boundaries are set on what is possible. It asks us to assume a different perspective, to invite new questions, and to be willing to be flexible. Creativity is not fixed but forever flowing like a river, continuously offering new nourishment for the soul.

History is filled with stories of creative geniuses who dared to challenge themselves with two little words, "What if?" Einstein constantly asked questions about the nature of light that moved him to think in new ways. Rather than remaining fixed on conventional ways of doing and thinking, simply asking "What if?" in the next minute can open the gates to creativity.

I used this approach to explore new ideas with Janet, a law clerk who tearfully described to me how she felt she wasn't reaching her potential and had disappointed her family. On the whiteboard in my office, I had Janet write the question "What if?" I asked her to write down beneath those words ideas of other kinds of work she could do. I also asked her not to censor or judge any of the ideas that came to mind, however silly or impractical she might find them or believed her family might judge them. I added this qualification of nonjudgment because creativity needs space to roam and play without being limited. An interesting trend appeared in Janet's answers: "a potter, a cake designer, a chef, a professional mountain climber, and a tour guide." She was surprised to discover two obvious themes, a strong interest in travel and the need for physical activity and working with her hands. For the first time, Janet started to entertain ideas for her own path, not the one others wanted for her.

The questions you ask yourself don't need to be life changing. You can inquire about any area where you find yourself stuck in a rut, or you can inquire within to tap into your storehouse of creativity for creativity's sake.

Creativity does not like to be forced, so asking a question and expecting the perfect answer in the next sixty seconds is counterproductive to the creative process. Two ways to enter into a more creative space in the next minute are to take a mental break and to change your physical location. Listen to music or take a short walk in nature. Let go of the issue you are trying to solve and allow your thoughts to flow as they will. Enjoy a one-minute breathing break. Burnout and overwork do not foster creativity.

Creativity flourishes in an atmosphere of support and enthusiasm. If there is a critic in your workplace or if you struggle with a "critic within," seek out a creative friend who is willing to look at new ideas with you. Most importantly, be your own creative best friend. A new minute is always unfolding in which you can affirm your creativity and the fresh ideas that come to you. Call upon patience and faith to be your creative friends too.

PRACTICE

Do one small creative thing at your workplace. Set your intention to do so the night before when you're going to sleep. Resolve to be flexible or to push past limits you've placed on yourself. You can also work with an affirmation, such as "The treasure of creativity is available to me at all times" or "I let go of expectation and let creativity come to me."

Escaping the Perfectionism Trap

Perfectionism is unforgiving. It demands nothing less than achieving total success by meeting the highest standards of excellence. To do less is to be mired in mediocrity and steeped in failure. Perfectionism offers the promise of control, leading us to believe that the bitter taste of loss and its accompaniments — disappointment, disapproval, and rejection — can be avoided.

The truth is we cannot avoid loss, no matter how perfect we try to be. But this truth is not a call to wave the slacker's flag, to do as little as possible, or to give up. Rigidly imposing impossibly high expectations on ourselves and others at all costs can actually make it harder to reach our goals. This kind of perspective and behavior affects our happiness. It is maladaptive. We're much better off when our desires to work hard and to pursue excellence are adaptive and flexible.

No one is immune to the perfectionism trap. I experienced its negative effects some years back when I presented a workshop on eating disorders. It was my first national conference, and I was determined to give my best workshop ever. Because of worry, though, I slept poorly the night before, and in an effort to make the presentation better, I shuffled materials around at the last moment, which left me no time to become familiar with the changes. After the presentation, only one person came up to talk with me, and the sinking feeling in my gut told me I had "failed."

Just after I left the room, I happened upon another speaker, happiness researcher Dr. Robert Biswas-Diener, who had just finished his own presentation. It was his first presentation at the conference too. "How did your talk go?" he asked me. "Not very well, I'm afraid. It wasn't near my best," I told him. "How about you?" I asked. Robert said that his talk hadn't gone as well as he had hoped, but he added, "I rate it a seven, and that's actually pretty good." When I asked what he meant, he shared his secret for working with perfectionism. He explained that realistically it's almost impossible to get a perfect ten on anything, so putting in an extra 20 to 30 percent of one's energy to make what is already good better or perfect is not worth it and is actually counterproductive. That time could be better spent. When he asked me to rate my presentation, I spent a moment reappraising my experience using his framework. "The truth is I covered all the material, even if it was a little disorganized and not as compelling as I would have liked," I told him. "I give it a seven." Robert smiled and said, "Seven is really ten." "Oh, so we both got tens," I replied. "What a relief!" We laughed.

Although I didn't get invited back to the conference, I didn't leave empty-handed. I learned a valuable lesson about *when good is good enough*. I also found that the instant I let go of my perfectionism and self-criticism, in the next minute my mood lifted dramatically. It's no surprise that researchers at the University of Oxford who examined studies on perfectionism concluded, "There is some indication that dysfunctional attitudes associated with perfectionism impede the successful treatment of depression."[15]

Do you need to let go of your grip on perfectionism? Reflect on your answers to the following questions:

- Do you delay starting projects because the outcome must be perfect?
- Similarly, do you delay completing projects because you worry the outcome won't be good enough?
- Do you worry excessively about how others will judge your work?
- Are you your own worst critic, always thinking you could have done better?
- Do you feel that any effort less than 100 percent is a failure?

PRACTICE

This is a two-part exercise. First, create your own definition of "failure" that takes into account the importance of learning and growing through mistakes and missteps. As long as we see failure as something terrible, we will continue to avoid it, but without failure as a teacher, we cannot fully mature and learn the grace of acceptance. This is why failure is a process that leads to the path of success. The next time you notice you are being critical of yourself or your work, take sixty seconds to reappraise your judgment using the one-to-ten scale where seven is really ten.

18.   Finding Pleasantness

*F*inding pleasantness is one of the easiest and most enjoyable activities in *One-Minute Mindfulness*. This practice is also one of the most profound. Shifting our awareness to what is pleasant and beautiful and good is deeply affirming. It taps into the fundamental goodness of life, and it helps us to master our attention. Without this vital skill, our attention is not ours but subject to distraction, disturbance, and any other nearby stimulation.

Pleasantness is an anchor that helps us center by locating the peace that is ever present, even when it is hidden. No matter how depressed or upset we might feel at a given moment, we have a brain that is wired to seek out pleasantness. It's a natural ability. I have yet to meet anyone — no matter how sad, depressed, or anxious — who could not find something in the next minute that was pleasing in some way. Whether a shape, a color, an object, there is always something.

When I first introduced the idea of pleasantness to Sally, a young woman in her twenties, she was a patient at an intensive outpatient psychiatric clinic. Recently released from the hospital for acute clinical depression, Sally had difficulty stabilizing her thoughts. She often either focused on her unhappy past or worried about the future, when she would return to a stressful job. As part of my pleasantness discussion, I asked all the members in Sally's therapy group to identify something they found pleasant. Sally said she liked nature, and later in the day, I noticed her smiling as she held an eye-catching yellow-and-red maple leaf. When I asked where she got it, Sally said she had found it near a tree during break. A group member suggested she laminate the leaf so that she could take it with her when she returned to work. The next day, Sally returned to group with the leaf beautifully laminated.

Keep in mind that pleasantness is not about ownership or possession, which can lead to grasping and craving and produce unpleasant feelings such as frustration, greed, lust, and envy. When we find what is pleasant, we focus our awareness on the essential beauty and basic decency in life in its myriad forms.

Also know that pleasantness does not need to be "big" or impressively awesome like the Grand Canyon. This practice is meant to uncover appreciation and delight in even the smallest things, such as the glistening green in a blade of grass. We can find pleasantness in a song or some other sound, in a favorite color, a graceful movement, or the elegant shape of an object. In the small café where I am writing these words, for example, I just spent the past minute noticing the green-and-brown slate flooring. The mottled pattern is soothing; it reminds me of water flowing in a stream. When I look outside, I see the fronds of tall palm trees waving in the wind, and when I inhale, I draw in the pleasant aromas of freshly toasted bread and freshly brewed coffee.

In the next minute, wherever you happen to be as you read this, scan your surroundings for anything you find pleasing. Appreciate what you find and know that you are deliberately and skillfully focusing your attention on what is good and lovely in life.

PRACTICE

To help you find peace whenever you need it in the workplace, bring an item that evokes pleasantness. This object can be a picture of someone or something you love, maybe a pet or a place you have visited or would like to visit. It's good to have something pleasant and meaningful that is portable as well, something you can carry with you and touch or look at when you need to feel calm and centered.

19. Gratitude for Work

*T*he practice of gratefulness is so important that I've included it in more than one section of this book. The word *gratitude* comes from the Latin word *gratitudo*, which means "to be thankful and to find pleasing." This original word is also linked to the blessing or grace that is said before or after a meal.

As discussed in chapter 9, "Gratitude for the Day," thankfulness is a practical and powerful means to shift our awareness and relieve depression. Gratitude in the workplace is vital for finding the meaning that counters life's hard knocks and our broken expectations of how things are "supposed to be."

Take the next minute to work with this exercise:

Imagine that you have worked and saved for more than thirty-five years, but just when you are preparing to retire, you lose most of your life savings to events out of your control. Faced with the need to work now for several more years, what would be your initial reaction?

This is exactly what happened to fifty-eight-year-old Ken, who had spent a lifetime working in the medical field. Ken's eyes were filled with tears when he described to me how he had poured all his life savings into designing and building a home at a remote location where he and his wife planned to enjoy their retirement. Over the years, he had done most of the construction himself. Then, just one month before they were going to move in, a deluge caused a landslide that destroyed both Ken's home and his retirement dream. The insurance would not cover the loss, leaving Ken devastated.

Some people would have given up and crawled into a hole of isolation and pity; others would have resented being forced to continue working. Ken and I talked about the good things he had accomplished in his life and how many people he had helped over the years. He also realized how fortunate it was that neither he nor his wife was in the house during the landslide. Gratitude did not erase the loss, but it did give Ken the strength to face the world again. He continued to work and focused on gratitude as he developed a new retirement plan. Gratitude helped Ken find his way back to a new dream.

How do you feel about the work you do each day? Do you appreciate all that work provides you, or do you wish you were somewhere else doing something else? Do you find ways to appreciate others, or do you feel like an outsider who doesn't fit in? Are you frustrated all day long because your efforts are underpaid and unacknowledged, or do you focus on giving the best of yourself? I am not recommending that you resign yourself to a job in which you are unappreciated or overwhelmed. By all means, seek out something more meaningful. But in the meantime, experiment with adopting a grateful perspective to see how it changes your experience. This choice is within your control, and since you're already at work, do you really want to add a burden of bitterness and suffering to your experience?

I am reminded of the Greek myth of Sisyphus, the king whose

punishment for tricking the gods was to push a boulder up a hill for eternity. Each time he got the boulder to the top, it rolled back down, and he had to push it back up again. If this is how you feel about your job, you need to find gratitude — and another job! Everyone has a boulder of some sort at work that needs pushing. When we resist the work, it pushes back and just feels heavier. Gratitude reduces the size of the rock and turns it into something we can move with less effort or maybe even jump over.

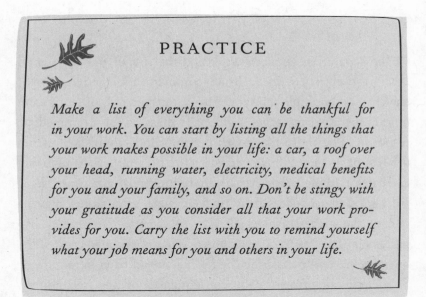

PRACTICE

Make a list of everything you can be thankful for in your work. You can start by listing all the things that your work makes possible in your life: a car, a roof over your head, running water, electricity, medical benefits for you and your family, and so on. Don't be stingy with your gratitude as you consider all that your work provides for you. Carry the list with you to remind yourself what your job means for you and others in your life.

20. Leaving Work Behind

*T*he separation between work and the rest of our lives is no longer clearly defined. Instant communication and the ease of travel across multiple time zones make the demands of work seem ubiquitous. Text messages and emails press us for an immediate response. The more that work becomes indistinguishable from the rest of our lives, however, the more difficult it is to maintain and safeguard the home as a sanctuary for repose and renewal.

Learning to successfully manage work after hours may be one of the great social challenges of twenty-first-century living. As far back as 1922, sociologist William Ogburn created the term *culture lag* to describe the problems and friction that occur as society catches up to the consequences of new technology. Ogburn believed that it could take up to fifty years to adapt to and manage the changes, and he added, "If the material culture should continue to accumulate and change with increasing rapidity, it would seem that the cultural lags will pile up even more."[16]

No one can tell you how to adapt to the demands and speed caused by an onslaught of technology. But you can choose to set boundaries minute by minute that honor what is most important to you in your life.

Letting go of work was unheard of for Stewart, a hardworking twenty-seven-year-old who came to see me because his relationship with his wife had become stale, empty, and lifeless. Stewart works as an engineer in the TV industry, and he was so devoted to his job that he refused to use his vacation days and remained on call during the weekends. When he came home from work, he typically cleaned the house, drank a six-pack of beer, or looked for a garage project. He rarely played his guitar or exercised. As a result, Stewart's wife also retreated into her job, working long hours into the weekends. When I asked Stewart what he wanted more than anything, he said, "I want to take a weekend off with my wife and take a short trip to the beach. But I don't know how."

Stewart's first step involved learning how to transition out of what his wife called his "workmania." To do this, he developed a specific transition practice that began in the first sixty seconds when he reached his car in the parking lot. During his ride home, he listened to soothing music, all the while reminding himself that work was over for the day. In the first sixty seconds of his arrival home, Stewart greeted his wife with a hug and a kiss. Next, he either took a hot shower or changed out of his work clothes. Then he spent up to thirty minutes alone, either practicing belly breathing to quiet his busy mind or using another practice to let go, such as running on his treadmill. Stewart also cut down on his drinking and tracked his moods each night. The results were dramatic. In just six weeks, Stewart and his wife were interacting more, and he was feeling hopeful for the first time in years. Stewart was beaming the day he shared with me the news that he and his wife were going to take a trip to the beach.

How do you transition after work? Do you live to work or

work to live? It helps to have a specific one-minute intention when you make the transition from work to home, something like the following:

With each unfolding minute upon entering my home,
may I discharge negative emotions.
May I cultivate patience.
May I wisely transition in order to bring
love, understanding, and tranquility into my home.

PRACTICE

Take a sheet of paper and draw a line down the middle. On the left-hand side, write down the behaviors that describe how you bring work home, and label this column "Bringing Work Home." Now label the right-hand column "Leaving Work Behind," and brainstorm strategies for leaving work behind. Have fun and be creative as you do this. You may even want to do this exercise as a shared family practice.

Part 3

RELATIONSHIPS AND LOVE

By embracing one-minute mindfulness in your relationships, you can strengthen trust, harmony, emotional connection, and peace. The small actions that each minute holds — the ability to listen, to show patience, to express empathy, and so on — are jewels, as valuable as any material gift. Let the following guidelines serve to enliven you and those you love.

21. Saying Hello with Love

*T*here is no small hello. The greetings we extend are no less vital and awe inspiring than the sunrise that illuminates and warms a new day. A simple greeting is not only a ritual that brings constancy to the day but also a powerful way to manifest love and to affirm that "everything is going to be all right."

Does your morning greeting spread warmth and support to others? Or does it spread indifference or anxiety? Take a minute to consider the following statements and identify the tone of your greetings.

- I am grumpy in the morning and want to be left alone.
- As soon as I wake up, I am thinking about all the things I have to do and already feel the anxiety building up.
- I don't usually kiss, touch, or hug others before leaving my home in the morning.
- When I arrive at work, I am all business. I get right to work and don't make an effort to talk to anyone other than with a quick "good morning."

If any of the statements above resonate with you, then you might find that a sixty-second shift in your greetings can build new bridges with those at home and at work.

There is probably nothing sadder than not being able to connect with someone you care about. When I first met forty-year-old Susan, a mother of two, she told me that the past two years of her life had been spent "in a cocoon of pain" because of chronic illness and painkillers. Although her health had improved recently, she explained, the cocoon of pain had erected a wall between her and her husband. It had also forced him to take on greater responsibilities at home. Not surprisingly, Susan's husband carried anger and hurt because of the situation.

Susan has started to rebuild this relationship by practicing nonverbal sixty-second greeting rituals, such as a smile, a kiss, a hug, or a light touch on her husband's shoulder. She also makes a point of verbally greeting her husband in the morning when she wakes up and when he comes home from work. Such rituals break the ice and eventually will allow Susan and her husband to share their feelings and move forward.

How do you greet your family at different times throughout the day? If you are a parent, how do you greet your children when they return from school? I know some harried parents who greet their children with a command to get their chores done. There is plenty of time for cleaning and homework, but the opportunity to greet your children only comes in those first moments. Greet your loved ones with care and respect.

PRACTICE

Changing your greeting routines may require some effort and appropriate motivation. Write down the various occasions for greeting others throughout your day — at home, at work, and elsewhere. Which of these greeting routines do you want to change? Write down specific verbal and nonverbal alternatives you can begin to use. Every time you remember to use one of these, do so without expecting anything in return. Simply know that you are spreading light, warmth, and hope, which is reason enough.

22. The Grace of Patience

*P*atience makes a mockery of expectations. It is the freedom to live at our own pace and in our own way. Patience is also an extraordinary grace that we extend to others in the most ordinary of circumstances. The patience we display in each minute makes the powerful statement that we are not judging others or ourselves harshly. With patience, we transcend all the annoying things life is known for.

Who or what has annoyed, irritated, or frustrated you today? Some studies indicate that as much as 10 percent of the population is irritated on a daily basis. This level of chronic annoyance may not be toxic or seriously harm others, but it can push people away and creates an atmosphere for negative emotions to escalate.

One of my favorite stories about annoyance involves the nineteenth-century mystic and teacher Gurdjieff, who attracted seekers to his training center outside Paris. Gurdjieff employed a crusty caretaker, who always managed to upset the students. One day they pulled such a nasty practical joke on the caretaker that he quit his job. When Gurdjieff heard of this, he located the man and not only begged him to return but also met his demands.

When the students were called to a meeting and learned about the caretaker's return, they expressed dismay. But Gurdjieff explained that the caretaker was one of his finest teachers, someone who pushed the students' buttons and forced them to look inward at their anger and disturbance.

One-minute mindfulness gives us the option to cool down and to extend the grace of patience to ourselves and others — in that immediate moment when we need it most. Patience is a form of forbearance, a value so important that it is among one of Buddhism's perfections on the path to enlightened living. Forbearance means we don't have to mindlessly react to annoyances and criticisms. It gives us the freedom to respond in a more spacious way. The Buddha outlined a one-minute mindfulness approach to patience when he explained to one of his monks, "There are profit and loss, slander and honor, praise and blame, pain and pleasure in this world; the Enlightened One is not controlled by these external things; they will cease as quickly as they come."[17]

In that first minute that follows an annoyance, remind yourself that the cause of your upset is impermanent. Think about the nature of what usually pushes you to the edge. Is the offending person, comment, or incident really a reflection of you? Does the annoyance go on and on, or does it stop at some point? If in that first minute you don't respond in your typical way, what will happen?

Forbearance and patience are necessary in all relationships to smooth over the little and bigger differences. Patience is not about someone walking all over you; it is a conscious decision to let things go. After all, we humans are subject to frailty. With one-minute patience in your corner, you can practice not taking the little things personally and use that experience to help you through the bigger upsets.

PRACTICE

For the next sixty seconds, visualize yourself in a difficult situation such as an argument. See yourself holding silence in response to the situation. While you see yourself this way, set the intention not to complain when your expectations are not met in various situations, such as when you're waiting in line, you're stuck in traffic, or someone criticizes you. Visualize yourself refraining from reacting negatively. The next time an upsetting event occurs, you will be ready to use what you have been mentally rehearsing. As you refrain from reacting, notice where in your body you feel irritation — the gut, the head, the chest — and with each exhalation, imagine the tension draining out of your hands and feet. You don't need to hold on to this for a minute longer.

23. Lighten Your Spirit

While material gifts can be nice, the one-minute mindfulness gifts of laughter and joy make a long-remembered and much-appreciated impact. Sharing our joy with others and supporting their happiness are skills we can easily bring to the next minute — and they cost nothing.

In *The Strengths Book*, authors Robert Biswas-Diener, Janet Willars, and Alex Linley identify sixty strengths for successful relationships. One of these is humor, which is described as "the ability to crack a joke or tell a story that lightens the mood, gives enjoyment to others, and helps people relax."[18] You don't need to be a stand-up comedian or quick with one-liners to be lighthearted; lightness of spirit can be cultivated. Simply seeing things from a fresh perspective in the next minute can help to transform a serious situation into a light one. I'm not suggesting that we disrespect or ignore the world's pain and sorrow, but we need the nourishment of looking on the brighter side of life whenever we can get it.

I don't have a good memory for jokes, but I do remember and appreciate the experience of shared laughter. I especially enjoy a hearty laugh with my clients. Whatever the cause, these moments are truly healing. Make it a point to seek out lightness and laughter wherever and whenever you can. For example, it takes only a minute to read a favorite comic strip in a newspaper. Political cartoons, which turn conventional thought and sacred cows upside down, are an excellent one-minute mindfulness method for remembering the irony in human behavior.

What do you take a bit too seriously in your life? Can you laugh at your own foibles and dissolve your egocentric focus? I had a friend who always wore a toupee to protect his image as a local TV news reporter. One morning when we met for breakfast, I couldn't help but notice that he was without his hairpiece. When I asked him about this, he told me about an incident on an airplane flight the previous week. He laid his head on the headrest to get some sleep, but his toupee got dislodged and slid forward over his forehead and eyes. It wasn't until the flight attendant came by asking for drink orders that he discovered what had happened. Instead of being embarrassed or ashamed, he laughed at himself. He decided then and there to remove the hairpiece and hasn't worn it since. Of course, laughing at our own foibles is different from laughing at someone else or being mean-spirited.

Another way to share positive feelings is to support another's path and success. If you're competitive or demanding of others, you'll miss the opportunity to experience this one-minute mindfulness gift. For example, if your child is happy to report earning the grade of a B, why shouldn't you be happy about it too? If a friend is excited to be learning about the plumbing trade, why insist that learning about medicine or law would be better? There are enough critical voices in this world; you don't have to be one of them. The gifts of joy and laughter you can share in the next minute will ripple out in ways you never imagined.

PRACTICE

Spend one day noticing and making a list of things you take a little too seriously, such as your appearance, your need to be perfect, your diet, job, grades, political beliefs, etc. Then make a conscious effort to lighten up, even a little bit, the minute you notice yourself taking these things too seriously again. Share your lighter observations and humor with others. Break the entrenched habits that keep you from experiencing laughter and joy.

24. Opening the Heart

*T*he heart has a language all its own. To speak from the heart in the next minute is to communicate from a place of love, truth, and beauty. But for many, the heart may be hidden and locked away behind a wall. To reveal the heart and its desires can be scary, yet to live without giving voice to the heart is like being mute and lost in the darkness. Open the heart, and we find not only help for ourselves but also the capacity to help others and share intimacy.

We would all do well to remember the one-minute mindfulness message that spiritual teacher Frank Coppieters shares when he writes, "Listen to what the heart has to say...it speaks in parables, songs, and visions. It gives you the courage to accomplish anything you desire. Such courage comes in spite of conditioning and can be experienced in this moment. Listen...the heart never lies."[19]

Have you listened to your heart lately? Take a minute with any one of the following questions to discover some of the secrets your heart wants to share:

- How can listening to my heart in the next sixty seconds help soften my view toward [fill in the blank]?
- What light of wisdom and truth does my heart have to shine on a difficult predicament I presently face?
- How can softening my heart allow me to accept others in my life?
- What feelings or words does my heart want to express in order to heal a relationship?

No matter how closed your heart may feel because of past loss or pain, you can always open it. Spend a minute recalling a time when your heart was soft, available, and present. This could have been a time when you held nothing back and did not worry about being vulnerable, perhaps with a friend, a lover, a grandparent, or even a pet. You could also think of a time when someone opened up to you. For example, when I was eight years old, I experienced the loving-kindness of elderly neighbors who lived in the same apartment building in Chicago. After school, I often knocked on their door with a big smile, hoping to visit with their dog, Mikey, a beautiful and loving Dalmatian. My heart was totally open to that dog and that couple who let me into their family.

It is also helpful to open the heart by visualizing your heart connected to a source of infinite love and light. If it helps, picture someone you know who embodies love and light — a favorite relative or a spiritual teacher — and imagine that person sending unconditional love into your heart center for a minute.

Don't give up on opening your heart, even a little at a time. An open heart is our natural state. From this place of abundance, where there is no worry or fear, the heart is willing to share and receive, to forgive and understand. In one minute of mindfulness, you can find the compassionate you in your heart. Whether you show your feelings through touch, words, or tears, know that tuning in to your heart will bring much needed hope and peace into the world.

PRACTICE

When the heart grows tender, it recognizes the precious-ness and fragility of each new minute. Throughout your day, find a minute here and there of silence and repose to get in touch with your heart. Be open to what you experi-ence. Remember that having an open heart means that you do not speak out of anger but that you find a kind and thoughtful way to express your feelings.

25. Listening Without Judgment

*T*o listen without judgment is a way to give nourishment to another. Just as a plant naturally turns toward the sunlight, we turn to someone who listens to us when we need the nourishment of a witness. Listening is an essential part of our narrative process, the process through which we share and cocreate the stories that bring meaning to our lives.

Listening is more than an element in communication. It is linked with healing in ways we are just beginning to understand. Lewis Mehl-Madrona, a psychiatrist who has studied the healing power of narrative, writes, "In my studies of extraordinary healing, I didn't encounter a single person who had healed in isolation.... People create systems that generate an energy field, which feeds back to make the people within the system more connected to each other and more coherent in their thoughts and feelings."[20]

But as you know, listening is not always easy. What roadblocks to listening do you face? See if any of the following statements describe times when it's been hard for you to lend an ear.

- I can't really listen when someone is trying to persuade, proselytize, or compete with me.
- I can't listen when I'm feeling upset or angry.
- I can't listen when I strongly disagree with the other person's point of view.
- I can't listen when I feel criticized, unheard, or disrespected.

Even in such trying moments as those mentioned above, listening is still possible. Listening doesn't mean we sit quietly, all the while lost in our thoughts or tuned out of what the other person is saying. Likewise, defending our thoughts can turn conversations into debates and battles of right and wrong. At such times, true listening will be diminished or lost. Listening is an accepting and nonjudgmental invitation for others to be themselves, without worry about disapproval. This is an extraordinary gift to offer another and may open the door to a deep mutual exploration of ideas and feelings.

One of the most powerful listening aids we possess is not our ears but our breath. Take several slow, calming breaths whenever you find yourself shutting down. Once you've calmed down, you will be better able to listen for the subtext — the emotional narrative beneath the words, the feeling that is telling you more about the content than the words alone. Asking questions to help you better understand another's point of view is also important and prevents multiple assumptions from getting in the way.

I once worked with Eddie, a man who avoided talking with his parents because of a lifetime of assumptions he had when listening to them. For example, he assumed that they were judging him as a parent, that they were imposing their religious values on him, and that they cared more about his children than him. When

Eddie was able to let go of assumptions, he could better hear that his parents cared about the well-being of the entire family.

PRACTICE

I call this exercise "Pause to Listen." It begins with a one-minute visualization that prepares you to be open and available to others. Imagine yourself meeting someone, either someone you know or someone you've just met, and picture yourself taking a long breath and listening without judgment to this person. You might want to try visualizing someone who makes you defensive. If you notice assumptions intruding, see if you can put them on the shelf during the next mindful minute of listening. During this practice session, stay centered on your breath. Listen without judgment, appreciating the uniqueness of the person standing before you. Instead of focusing only on the verbal content, notice the feelings beneath the words. When you listen in this way, you make a choice to accept the person, though not necessarily the message or information being expressed. If you find that you have stopped really listening, begin the process again. After mentally rehearsing this, try this for real.

26. Plant Seeds of Friendship

*I*t goes without saying that harming others does not a friendly community make. With one-minute mindfulness, we can begin to refrain from doing harm while cultivating love and good relations. When we live with this value, we honor all with whom we share the air and other natural resources, as well as all those who will inherit the seeds we plant today. Such is the sentiment echoed in my poem "Friendship Field."[21]

Each spring I plant a friendship field
with seeds of loving-kindness.

Every day I nurture my field
with caring words, actions, joys, and hopes.
I water it often with
compassionate action and laughter.

Come harvest time,
my field overflows with enough friendship
to warm and sustain me,

during even the darkest,
coldest winter.

Here are four ways in which you can mindfully plant your own friendship field one minute at a time. First, notice your negative impulses, which means accepting and recognizing that you can't force yourself to be kind and loving all of the time. Even Mother Teresa's path was filled with doubt. If you notice a harmful emotion or thought, take a minute to breathe and investigate what caused it. Remind yourself that you're doing the best you can.

Second, spend a minute saying a prayer for a difficult person or situation in your life. When we pray for others, we feel compassion for the circumstances that make them who they are. This may help you gain more understanding and empathy.

Third, plant seeds of friendship by helping and cherishing others, even in little ways. It is the small actions that let others know they are loved and valued, and small actions only take a minue. Take to heart the words of Robert Louis Stevenson, who wrote in a letter, "It is the history of our kindnesses that alone makes this world tolerable. If it were not for that, for the effect of kind words, kind looks, kind letters...I should be inclined to think our life a practical jest in the worst possible spirit."[22]

Finally, strive to let go of your expectations about the way people should act. Instead of getting frustrated, accept that all individuals are imperfect and subject to ignorance, confusion, and delusion. Then give as much as you feel capable of giving from your heart, without demanding anything in return. Give freely to others. And you never know from what direction friendship may come, so plant one-minute seeds of love and kindness wherever you happen to be.

PRACTICE

Make a list of the qualities you feel are important for developing friendship, such as loyalty, dependability, listening, trust, acceptance, and so on. Embody these qualities one minute at a time to cultivate and grow your friendship field.

27. Trust and Transparency

*T*rust is the lifeblood of relationships; it reinvigorates them with every nourishing interaction. Trust begins with transparency, the ways in which we are direct and truthful in relationship, and it is sustained when we honor our commitments. Wise speech also plays a critical role in creating and nurturing trust. Unkind, thoughtless speech creates pain, mistrust, and separation.

If you have ever been on the receiving end of dishonesty, a broken promise, or abusive speech (and who hasn't?), you know how these betrayals damage a relationship. But instead of dwelling on the erosion of trust, we can choose to focus on creating trust. The following principles offer helpful guidance.

Clarity and transparency have a curative effect. When we keep a secret, we feel dishonest, but when we make our real feelings known, we live authentically and lower the possibility of harming another. To become more transparent, ask yourself these questions:

- What do I fear by being more transparent? What holds me back?

- How can I be more straightforward and less manipulative?
- What is the best thing that can come from being more direct?

Commitments are the actions that back up our words and vows. Without committed action, our words are meaningless and trust is weakened. When you make a plan to be somewhere or to do something with someone, do you follow through, or do you back out at the last minute because something more appealing came your way? Keeping our commitments demonstrates how much we value a relationship. These questions can provide you with more clarity:

- How often do I stick to my relationship commitments, respecting the time and the energy they require?
- Do I show up when I say I'm going to?
- In the next minute, do any changes come to mind that would strengthen a commitment?

Wise speech is the currency that forges long-lasting bonds. The timing of our speech is important. Is the next minute the best time to say what's on our mind? Sometimes not speaking is critical, especially when we are upset and reactive. Although it is important to express our feelings, if we cannot speak calmly, then it's wise to wait until we can. When we speak in a respectful, nonblaming, and nonjudgmental way, even if we don't agree with another, it supports everyone's being heard and understood. Of course, being skillful with our words means speaking honestly and beneficially, not resorting to gossip or manipulation. When we use words as a weapon, we jeopardize cooperation and collaboration. Honesty doesn't mean we have to disguise our personal truth, but at the same time, it doesn't mean being unkind or mean-spirited.

Consider how you can bring one-minute mindfulness to the following issues:

- How can I express what I need to share with kindness and respect?
- How can I let go of obstacles to honesty, such as envy, greed, and self-interest?
- How can I use my words to express my deeper values?

Technology is rapidly transforming how we relate to one another. Increasingly, we don't share face-to-face interactions, but the same principles for creating trust apply to our behavior when we are texting, emailing, chatting, Facebooking, and using all the other forms of digital communication.

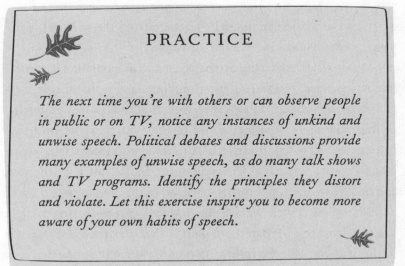

PRACTICE

The next time you're with others or can observe people in public or on TV, notice any instances of unkind and unwise speech. Political debates and discussions provide many examples of unwise speech, as do many talk shows and TV programs. Identify the principles they distort and violate. Let this exercise inspire you to become more aware of your own habits of speech.

$\mathcal{28.}$ Finding Forgiveness

Wisdom traditions are filled with parables of forgiveness and stories about the importance of "turning the other cheek." Buddhist teacher Jack Kornfield advises, "To forgive does not mean we condone the misdeeds of another. We can dedicate ourselves to making sure they never happen again. But without forgiveness the world can never be released from the sorrows of the past.... Forgiveness is a way to move on."[23]

My experience as a psychotherapist and as a human being who has experienced injustice up close and personal is that forgiveness is a steep and rocky landscape to trek. There is something compelling, perhaps validating, about reciting our story of mistreatment over and over. In the long run, though, it doesn't serve our best interests, because it leaves us stuck in the muck of the past and unable to unwrap the gifts enfolded in the next minute.

The good news? We are the warden who possesses the key to the prison cell of anger and pain, so we can walk out into the sunlight again. Use the following one-minute mindfulness inventory to contemplate the possibility of freeing yourself from hurts and grievances.

- What is the depth of my anger and sorrow? How are they affecting my life?
- What is the worst thing that would happen if in the next minute I decided to let go of my anger? Even some of my anger?
- Maybe the person who harmed me doesn't deserve forgiveness, but how would forgiveness benefit me and my other relationships?
- How does holding on to the story of anger and victimization make me feel? What would it mean to let go of this story?

Forgiveness does not mean we forget a violation or injustice and allow it to reappear in our lives. However, every story has many perspectives, and it may be that the truth of our story can reveal our strength, not just our weakness and vulnerability. Viktor Frankl's five years in Auschwitz and other concentration camps could have buried him in a personal story of abuse, bitterness, and anger. Instead, he used the experience to write *Man's Search for Meaning*, a book about finding purpose and meaning in life's most difficult circumstances. Even when Frankl was close to death in a concentration camp, he did not dwell on the horrific circumstances but maintained a focus on his strengths and his desire to complete his manuscript, and this kept him alive.[24]

What is the alternate story of your experience, and what does it reveal about you? What strengths have you developed? Difficult experiences often call upon our tenacity, hope, cooperation, resourcefulness, adaptability, belief in ourselves, commitment to a goal or a purpose, love, generosity, and compassion, as well as our humor, among other qualities. To this list, we can add the strength of extending forgiveness.

When you focus on your strengths, how does it make you feel? What story line can you focus on to find peace as you move your life forward? Forgiveness is an extraordinary gift we give to ourselves and others. No one can grant forgiveness except you, which makes it not only powerful but also empowering.

PRACTICE

One of the best places to begin to extend forgiveness is to yourself. Use the words below to gently let go of guilt and pain in this one-minute forgiveness practice. No one is immune from being hurt or from hurting others.

May I forgive myself for harming another,
either intentionally or unintentionally.
May I forgive others who have harmed me,
either intentionally or unintentionally.
May I forgive myself for harming myself,
either intentionally or unintentionally.

29. Letting It Be

*L*ife and relationships can get messy. We can either let a mess stick to us or find a way to let it drop off and regain peace and clarity. Why do things stick? Most of us get strongly attached to an idea, a role, a point of view, or a belief. A one-minute mindfulness approach for letting things be can change this and make it easier to clean up after any mess.

In his book *The Lotus Effect*, psychologist Pavel Somov describes how the lotus flower's unique water-repellent properties allow it to emerge above water in pristine condition, untainted by the muddy depths from which it grows. According to Somov, "The sacred lotus offers an inspiring rags-to-riches, slime-to-sunshine metaphor of growth and enlightenment....It manages to remain *itself*, pure and unaffected, and to grow to its fullest amidst the impurity of its circumstance."[25]

Letting it be is a lotus-like method of self-cleansing and freeing yourself from your own sticky nature — those things you strongly identify with and cling to for dear life. Do you, for example, adhere to a rigid script of *shoulds*? How a lover, partner, father, mother, or child is supposed to act? You know the sticky scripts: it's the woman's job to clean the house, the man is the head of the household, or children should be seen and not heard. Strangely, these scripts may not even be your own; rather, you inherited them and have yet to consciously evaluate them. Take a minute now to begin reflecting on the following important questions:

- What roles have I inherited from my family and culture that I cling to without question?
- How do my unquestioned beliefs, behaviors, attitudes, or roles cause me and others pain?
- What would happen if for one minute I chose not to hold on to my view and let things be otherwise?
- What would happen if I let go of my need to control this relationship?

Letting it be also means we don't have to take everything so personally, and it means we can surrender the notion that we can control everything in our lives. No one can. Controlling takes an immense amount of energy, and since we can't control everything, is it really worth the effort?

When you recognize the painful consequences of holding on to something, letting go or letting it be becomes easier. To let it be is to loosen your grip and not hold on so tightly. Letting it be means you can take a breather from any situation. It brings clarity and insight into the meaning of surrendering the ego and the self's desires. It lets you respond from your wiser and more spacious self, not from the limited and fearful self.

It's also important to remember that letting it be doesn't mean you don't care. It's just that you are no longer invested in building a brick wall to keep things from changing or to enforce your view. In *The Sacred Tree*, a book about Native American spirituality, Judie Bopp explains, "To let go of something (like knowledge or love or hate) is not to throw it away. It is to step outside its shadow so that things may be seen in a different light."[26] To live in this way is to resemble a cloud — floating, alive, and able to move freely in each new, dynamic minute.

PRACTICE

For one minute during the day, let go of one belief or behavior that you typically cling to. If you always eat all the food on your plate, leave some and learn how to let it be. If you normally expect your partner to do something a certain way, try to take on the task yourself or surrender to the way it is even if you don't feel it's as it should be. Let it be. Every day, let one more thing be, just for the fun of it.

30. Goodbye for Now

Just as there is no small hello, there is no small goodbye. Every goodbye holds the seed of a new and fruitful greeting. Saying farewell can be a conscious act of separation that engenders love, togetherness, reliability, and wholeness. How we choose to say goodbye affects the energy and enthusiasm we bring to the day. A goodbye is a meaningful and vital ritual. After all, it makes a lasting impression.

How you say goodbye is a barometer that measures the health of your relationships. I worked with one couple, Paul and Kim, who both said they felt ignored by the other. When I asked each of them to name one small behavior the other person could perform on a daily basis to change the dynamic, they asked for a different goodbye ritual. Kim wanted Paul to give her a goodnight kiss and a wish for sweet dreams, and Paul wanted a hug before he went off to work in the morning. I was glad they included touch in their ritual. Touch stimulates the production of oxytocin, a hormone that creates feelings of bonding and intimacy. These small changes required Paul to adjust his sleep time so he could say goodnight, while Kim needed to climb out of bed earlier each morning to give Paul his goodbye hug. Although these rituals felt a little forced at first, a sense of closeness was restored.

Don't underestimate the importance of saying goodbye. It is not uncommon for many people to experience anxiety and discomfort during times of daily separation. This is especially true for those who grew up with parents or caregivers who were inattentive or neglectful and caused them to feel unsafe or insecure. For these people, even a temporary separation from someone close can be felt as a loss. A thoughtful goodbye ritual can be beneficial.

Use the questions below to shed light on your own goodbye behaviors and attitudes.

- In the morning, do you pause to acknowledge your loved ones before leaving for the day? Do you use touch to express closeness?
- Do you show an interest in loved ones by asking about their upcoming day?
- Do you remember to mention what time you expect to return home?
- Do you wish each other well? Do you share a moment of connection in the form of a kiss, a hug, a wave, a kind word, or a smile?
- Does your morning ritual leave you feeling good, or does it leave you feeling empty or ignored?
- Going to sleep is a time of separation too. How do you say goodnight to your loved ones?

I'm not saying that your morning goodbye ritual has to be a sit-down with tea, scones, and orange juice (although that's not a bad thing). What matters is that your goodbye serve as a faithful touchstone that enhances togetherness and affirms the relationship.

PRACTICE

Pause for one minute as you prepare to leave today (from home, work, the grocery store, wherever) and consider how you can bring sensitivity and joy into this transition. How can you bring your full presence into your next goodbye?

Create a "goodbye journal" that describes the day's partings. Were they memorable? Did they express your gratitude for the experience you had? Did they contain the seeds of your future greeting? Were they rushed and intense or easy and tranquil?

Part 4

One-Minute Mindfulness for

HEALTH AND
WELL-BEING

To fully realize the benefits of one-minute mindfulness, making your own physical and emotional health a priority is vital. Personal well-being is attained by bringing a set of centering and soothing skills into your life. With one-minute mindfulness, you can use the next sixty seconds to regulate your body and emotions for peace, clarity, and calm.

31. Morning Care

The choices we make every waking minute are a statement of how well we care for ourselves. Morning presents us with an opportunity to cultivate inner hospitality. Even if the morning feels like a frantic blur, small preparations and beneficial activities go a long way toward preparing mind and body for the day ahead.

It's easy to underestimate all the good things we do for ourselves in the morning. Simply noticing gestures of self-kindness we already practice can be an important step toward developing a greater awareness of our morning care. Use the next minute to take a personal inventory of the six beneficial behaviors that follow:

BODY CARE

- Brushing your teeth, showering, and general hygiene
- Moving, stretching, and exercising
- Eating nutritious food

MIND CARE

- Choosing clothes to help you feel good about your appearance

- Focusing with an intention, a meditation, or a centering practice
- Minimizing negativity and anxiety-producing stimuli

If you regularly practice two of the body-care and two of the mind-care activities listed above, you are devoting valuable time to your morning care, even if you didn't think so. Which of the morning practices tend to slide under your radar? How would it feel if you were to find time for these nurturing activities? What obstacles prevent you from doing so?

Monica was a stressed-out thirty-five-year-old mother of three, who came to see me because of her workload, which included managing the household, driving the children to various classes and activities, and a part-time job. Not surprisingly, Monica felt increasingly exhausted and irritated. When she took the morning-care inventory, she was surprised to find that she was actually taking pretty good care of herself. Encouraged, she went on to pay attention to those areas she could improve upon, such as taking care of her body and reducing anxiety. She added some simple stretches after her shower, which took little time, and she asked her husband to help shuttle the children. These changes made her feel supported, gave her extra energy, and improved her overall health.

Mindful one-minute changes in morning care don't require a full aerobic workout, a sit-down breakfast, or thirty minutes of meditation. Small, realistic, and meaningful choices make a noticeable difference. Gently stretching for a few minutes, eating a hard-boiled egg or cereal, and consciously affirming positive intentions demonstrate how you feel about yourself and your willingness to make self-care a priority. May each beneficial action inspire every minute of your day.

PRACTICE

To become more aware of your morning-care behaviors, keep a "morning-care journal." One way to do this is to create two columns on a page and write "Beneficial" above one column and "Unbeneficial" above the other. Use the examples in this chapter to help you identify activities and boundaries for each category. Skipping breakfast would clearly go in the Unbeneficial column. You may discover that you are already nurturing your-self more than you imagined. Take a minute now to con-sider what else you might do.

32. Inward Smile

When was the last time you thanked your body for all it does for you on a daily basis? The "inward smile" is an ancient practice, a way to deeply honor the body by acknowledging it and sending it gratitude. It's also a practice you can begin in the next minute. The inward smile goes by names such as the "cosmic smile," the "universal smile," and, in mindfulness-based stress reduction parlance, the "body scan." That it is part of so many traditions is testimony to its significance.

When we smile inwardly at the body, we change our relationship with it in a positive and tangible way. To discover how this practice can help you, take a minute to reflect on these questions:

- Do you often criticize your body or compare it to others'?
- Are you angry because your body is not taller, shorter, thinner, or [fill in the blank]?
- When looking in the mirror, do you focus on what you consider your flaws?
- Do you blame yourself for having harmed your body in some way, such as through past actions, risky behaviors, substance use, etc.?

I have found the inward smile an ideal morning practice to counter negativity and turn the mind in a positive direction at the start of the day, though it can be used anytime during the day. This practice activates the motor and sensory cortex of the brain — it's kind of like massaging the brain from the inside out. It also introduces a centering practice into your life that strengthens personal qualities such as self-discipline and self-restraint. Discipline is sometimes mistakenly viewed as dampening joy, but as Buddhist monk Bhante Henepola Gunaratana points out, "A well-disciplined life can also be a source of happiness."[27]

Let's review the practice of the inward smile. The purpose of this practice is to sense the body directly, without the mind jumping in to label a feeling "pleasant" or "unpleasant." In truth, a sensation itself has no name; it is just the momentary feeling that exists. A sensation does not define who you are. You will simply be observing, directly and without interfering thoughts, whatever signals are present in a part of the body.

Begin by taking a few moments to feel grateful for your body, this extraordinary gift you possess. Then, starting at your feet and working your way up to your head, place your attention on each part of the body. As you notice your feet, bring all of your awareness to them, from the back of the feet to the tips of the toes. Notice the sensation that arises in the moment — and in the next moment. After noticing a part of the body, smile inwardly at that part by sending it your deep gratitude. Think of all it does for you on a daily basis. Your feet, for example, allow you to walk, to drive your car, to wash in the shower, and they do all that they do without complaint. Marvelous, isn't it?

You can spend as much time as you want noticing sensations and sending gratitude to each part of the body, from the feet to the legs, to the torso, arms, hands, spine, internal organs, neck, face, and brain. If you notice pain or discomfort anywhere or if you have experienced trauma in a particular part of the body, you can focus on sending relief to that area or move on and return to the painful area later. Because you are in control, you can also take a break when you experience any discomfort. After you have completed the body scan and brought an inward smile to the body's various parts, rest in the knowledge that your body helps you accomplish your goals every day.

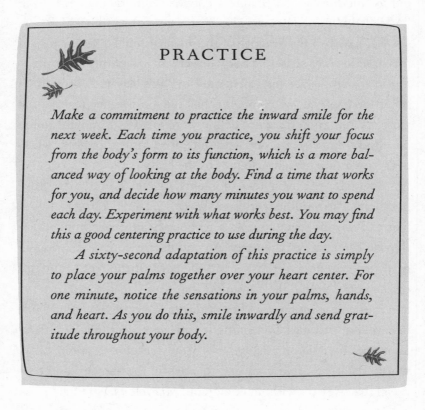

PRACTICE

Make a commitment to practice the inward smile for the next week. Each time you practice, you shift your focus from the body's form to its function, which is a more balanced way of looking at the body. Find a time that works for you, and decide how many minutes you want to spend each day. Experiment with what works best. You may find this a good centering practice to use during the day.

A sixty-second adaptation of this practice is simply to place your palms together over your heart center. For one minute, notice the sensations in your palms, hands, and heart. As you do this, smile inwardly and send gratitude throughout your body.

33. Heeding Signals from Within

The body is the perfect traffic signal. It tells us when to safely proceed, when to pause or slow down, and when to stop. To find balance and harmony in our lives, all we have to do is attend to these signals. Although it sounds easy, it isn't always that simple. Often the mind overlooks these signals and disregards the body's innate wisdom.

What signals is your body sending you in this moment? What are its warning signs telling you, that you may be stuck and out of balance? How can you tell when a change needs to be made? Questions such as these can help you begin to tune in to the body's messages, its signs of tiredness, hunger, pain, and tension, among others. Do you need to rest? Do you need to work less and enjoy yourself more? Do you have a nagging physical pain or problem that you have been ignoring? Is your body telling you to seek professional help? Perhaps the most important question of all is, What can I do in the next minute to respond to the message my body is sending? You may not be able to remedy the situation in one minute, but you can face it and vow to do something about it.

Physical sensations are only one aspect of heeding signals

from within. We can also pay attention to emotions and feelings in the body associated with our emotions, whether sadness, hurt, anger, frustration, anxiety, and so forth. Sometimes it's hard to admit that a job or a relationship is not working. I've encountered several people whose jobs had them in tears or dealing with anxiety attacks on an almost-daily basis. Still, many of them did not want to admit or accept that these were obvious signals demanding they do something about their stress levels.

What are your automatic reactions to stress? In *Heal Your Mind, Rewire Your Brain*, meditator and therapist Patt Lind-Kyle points out, "The real problem is that we fail to identify the true source of our stress, instead blaming everything from the president to the neighbor's barking dog for the tense state in which we find ourselves. We don't realize that, in fact, we are the culprit, that our stress stems from our social programming and our automatic reactions."[28] In these next few moments, you can begin to reprogram your mind and body simply by being present with the truth of what you are feeling or experiencing.

Don't ignore your body's messages. Instead, take a few soothing and calming breaths as you sit with whatever you're feeling. With each exhalation, imagine letting the stress drain through your body and out through the bottom of your feet. Picture the body becoming more relaxed. You do not need to solve the problem; just allow yourself to be more aware, present, and flexible in the moment. As you grow more calm and relaxed, you may find that you have more insight into the situation you face.

PRACTICE

Make a list of the different signals your body sends you in different areas of your life. Get to know which signals mean "go," which mean "pause," and which mean "stop." The more familiar you are with the signals, the more prepared you will be to respond to a signal the minute you notice it, with calm and acceptance.

34. At Peace with Desire

Appetite is not just physical. Desire speaks in many languages, but like a hungry ghost it demands more and often leaves us dissatisfied, no matter how voraciously we try to satisfy ourselves. Some desires are wholesome, such as seeking security, companionship, and meaning, but unhealthy desires such as jealousy, greed, and lust drive us into unhappiness and suffering. Knowing the difference between our healthy and unhealthy desires can lead to greater peace and clarity in the next minute.

In Buddhist lore, a hungry ghost is a being with a huge belly, a large mouth, and a mighty appetite. But the hungry ghost has a narrow, slender throat, which makes satisfying its immense hunger impossible. Trying to satisfy the hungry ghost within ourselves through constant feeding can provide only a little temporary relief. It doesn't address the root cause of the desire. For example, emotional eating is not about food. With emotional eating, it's not what we're eating but what's eating us that really matters. A more productive and healing way to work with a desire that produces pain and suffering is to become friends with our hungry ghost. When we take it under our wing with compassion and love, a hungry ghost can guide us to the root of its desire and its remedy.

Right now, take a few healing breaths, and then review the following questions to take inventory of any hungry ghosts in your life.

• Do you frequently eat to escape uncomfortable feelings or boredom?

• Do you often shop to make yourself feel better, whether or not you can afford to?

• Do you find that your achievements, jobs, or relationships ultimately leave you unsatisfied and wanting new ones that are "better"?

• Do you measure your worth by what and how much you have — money, cars, and the other trappings of success?

Susan Albers, an expert on hunger and eating, writes, "If you think you can calm yourself down without food, you will act in ways that will help you do exactly that. If you don't think it's possible, you won't even try. For this reason, your thoughts hold an enormous amount of power."[29] Because thoughts shape the networks in our brains, using affirmations can help us tap into the wholeness that satisfies unhealthy desires. Affirmations like the ones below can move you beyond cravings so that they don't rule your life. See if any of the following make sense for you.

• I am doing the best I can. I am successful just as I am.

• More [fill in the blank] will not make me a better person.

• I am worthy of love and support right now.

• I notice my desires and hungry ghosts without giving in to them. I can find true support, comfort, and encouragement in the next minute by [fill in the blank].

Create several of your own affirmations; perhaps write them on an index card that you can carry with you. Say your affirmations frequently and the minute a hungry ghost appears.

PRACTICE

Identify the deeper feeling your hungry ghost is covering up. If the feeling is loneliness, do what you can to make connections with others instead of pursuing empty activities to temporarily distract yourself from the truth. If your hungry ghost is covering up sadness, loss, or grief, find a truthful and fruitful way to work through such feelings. You might volunteer somewhere or explore a spiritual path. Make a list of productive, supportive activities that can take the place of unhelpful fixes for your hungry ghost's appetite.

35. Be the Pebble

*A*n anxious mind can be as turbulent as a raging river. Thoughts arise with such intensity and frequency that they can produce feelings of panic, upset, and nausea. It's like clinging to a log and rushing toward the roaring falls with no rescue in sight. Fortunately, there is a lifesaver that can transport us away from the raging waters to a place of peace and stillness beneath the waves.

To reach this protected and secure place, you need to find a word that you will use to act like a pebble that drops into and beneath the roiling water. The word will carry you into the stillness below the surface of conscious thought. It will let you rest at the bottom, unbothered by the wild waves above. You can choose a word or a phrase to focus your attention beneath the surface of anxious or ruminating thoughts. This word can be anything that helps you focus without stirring up distracting memories, associations, or emotions. The pebble's purpose is to distance you from the turbulence and settle you into the deep, still water, where you can see all around clearly. Take a minute to see if any of the neutral words below connect with you. Your own word may just pop into your mind, and if this happens, wonderful! You can always try a word out for now and choose another later.

one
pebble
peace
neutral
calm

After you've chosen a word, find a quiet place where you can sit. You can use the following pebble meditation for a minute or longer if you want. Many people practice this for ten or twenty minutes a day. Simply say your word mentally, in an easy, unforced way. Other thoughts will naturally occur as you focus on the word. Watch them as if they were shiny, interesting fish swimming past you. Just notice and continue to be present with your word. If uncomfortable feelings arise, your mind will be drawn to them, as it is with other thoughts. Usually these will dissipate and swim away. If you feel too upset for any reason, you can open your eyes and try another time. Remember that you are always in control. Pleasant feelings may also arise, and you can watch these too until they swim past. Don't try to hold on to any feelings or expect this exercise to be the same each time you try it. Just let yourself rest in the silence. See if this doesn't help you quiet your anxious mind after sixty seconds.

Suppose for a moment you could listen in on the thoughts of an anxious person. What do you think you would hear? Would you take the ramblings seriously, or would you recognize that such thoughts are the products of an anxious mind doing what it does — generating thoughts? Likewise, your thoughts are not you, but because they come from within your own head, you believe them.

PRACTICE

You can use the pebble meditation any time you feel anxious, stressed, or upset. You might also want to make a commitment to practice it once a day. Make a note of your anxiety level, rating it on a one-to-ten scale, before and after you practice. In this way, you can learn how many minutes work best for you while you gather evidence that this practice does indeed help you find calm and clarity.

36. Exercise the Brain and the Body

*L*ong before there was a Walmart, Costco, Sam's Club, or fast-food establishment on every corner, humans trekked for miles and hours a day to find their food. Walking and physical movement are woven into our ancestry and lore. Ancient traditions that still persist, such as the Australian Aborigines' walkabout, echo the human need to discover oneself and one's cultural and spiritual legacy through movement. The ancient brain and nervous system have not changed much in the past hundred thousand years. And if anything like an elixir of youth exists, it would have to be exercise. No pharmaceutical on the market can produce the same enhancing effects on the brain and the body. If you have thought about exercise but haven't yet committed to it, know that scientific evidence of its importance is mounting in almost every conceivable area of life.

In *Spark*, a book about how exercise stimulates the brain, clinical professor of psychiatry John Ratey writes, "What neuroscientists have discovered in the past five years alone paints a riveting picture of the biological relationship between the body, the brain, and the mind...and why physical activity is crucial to the way we think and feel."[30] Exercise is vital for learning because it produces a substance known as "brain-derived neurotrophic factor," or BDNF, which encourages neurons to grow and make connections and protects the parts of the brain associated with learning and emotional control. Exercise during the next minute, and you will begin to stimulate the production of a host of neurotransmitters and hormones that safeguard against anxiety, depression, ADHD, dementia, aging, and obesity. (Sorry, but it won't prevent baldness, as least as far as we know.)

Modern technologies and conveniences have disrupted opportunities for us to regularly exercise. There is no need to train for a marathon, though; even moderate and mild exercise are beneficial. For example, according to David Nieman, a researcher and the chairman of Loma Linda University's health science department, "Walking seems to prime the immune system so that it's ready for action."[31] If you don't exercise enough, finding a way to begin is most important. What simple choices can you think of in the next minute to get you moving? You could park your car farther from your destination or take the stairs instead of the elevator for starters. Take a minute to visualize yourself acting on your decision to move a little more.

Instead of following the old scripts — I don't have enough time, I'm not in good-enough condition to start exercising, or I'm too [fill in the blank] to start now — create a new script. It only takes a minute. Here are a few examples to get you started:

- I want to have more energy, and even a little bit of exercise will help.
- I might enjoy exercising, so I will try it.
- I can follow an exercise plan that works specifically for me.

PRACTICE

A good way to start exercising is to commit to a schedule. In the next minute, write down when, where, and how long you will engage in some form of exercise. Walking the dog most definitely qualifies as exercise, and some housework, such as vacuuming, qualifies as mild exercise. Also tell a friend about your plan so that you can be accountable. It only takes a minute of mindfulness to create a one-week plan for exercising. At the end of the week, you can modify your plan if you need to. Eventually, you can create a one-month plan, and after a month, you can design another one-month plan. Experiment with exercise times and routines. You are always in control and can revise the plan. Just beware of those excuses for not exercising!

37. Eating Moderately

*I*n the past one hundred years, eating habits have altered dramatically in many cultures. Obesity and other eating disorders have surged; they are a national health concern in the United States. Sugar consumption from the years 1900 to 2000 skyrocketed from an average of five teaspoons a day to nearly a half pound of sugar daily per person — that's 158 pounds of sugar a year![32] Processed foods have become more the rule than the exception, and eating has become more of an afterthought than a means to nourish and sustain the individual, much less the family and the community.

How can we return to a place of moderation, mindfulness, and harmony with food? The secret is how we think about our food. You're less moved to eat something right after you've eaten, right? New research shows that we also will eat less of a food if we simply *imagine* eating it. Participants in a study became habituated to a food they imagined eating, and as a result, their desire for that food (even candy) was significantly reduced.[33]

This research is consistent with what I've seen happen when I teach mindful eating and ask individuals to pay careful attention to eating a raisin for anywhere from five to ten minutes. They experience a raisin as they never have before, getting to know and savor all its aspects. When I ask if anyone would like a second raisin at the end of the exercise, believe it or not, sometimes someone will answer, "I'd have another, but I'm feeling very full." I have emotional eaters do this exercise with the "forbidden foods" they tend to binge on. They hold a small portion of the food in their hands, feel its weight, and notice its color and texture. They spend time sensing its aroma and noticing any memories this triggers. Then they reflect on how this particular food made it to the market — how it was tended to, packaged, and shipped. Finally, they slowly savor the food in their mouth, noticing how the flavor and consistency change with each chew.

Try this mindful-eating exercise with a slice of orange, a small square of chocolate, a single potato chip, or some other food. Notice your level of hunger before and after you do this. I suggest taking at least five minutes to eat a single morsel. This exercise is a form of mental rehearsal that trains you to eat more mindfully in general. You may discover that you don't need as much food or drink as you've previously thought. The next time you're about to eat, take a minute to visualize yourself eating slowly, with dignity and grace. Imagine yourself eating just enough food and then leaving the table feeling satisfied and content.

PRACTICE

Pay attention to your feelings as you approach your next meal. Are you nervous, angry, bored, stressed out? How you enter your meal can lead to unbalanced eating. Spend the next minute discharging any negative energy, perhaps by taking some deep breaths. Rate your hunger level and think about how much food would satisfy this hunger. Also, make a habit of leaving a little food on your plate. This can help you feel that there is an abundance of food available to you. You don't need to finish it all because there will be another meal to enjoy.

38. Recognize Resources

S ustainable resources are not only what help us get better gas mileage, power the water heater, and reduce landfills. Sustainable resources are also what renew our spirit, and many of these are available to you in the next sixty seconds, because they are much closer than you might imagine.

When Jane first came to see me, her life was in total flux. She had just moved away from her family in the Northeast, her marriage was on shaky ground, and she was struggling to move her career forward. To make matters worse, a temporary office job failed to alleviate financial woes. With each new setback, Jane repeated her sad refrain, "I am stuck, and I don't see a way out." To keep her from losing faith, I gave Jane an assignment to find individuals who could give her evidence that people do bounce back from hardships. Jane made an effort to contact old and new friends, and they shared their stories. Additionally, although she had resisted asking her family for support, Jane was delighted to find that when she did, they called more frequently. They even chipped in for airfare so she could visit during the holidays. Jane watched inspiring films such as *Norma Rae* and *A League of Their Own*, which depict strong women overcoming struggles by making bold, liberating, and imaginative life choices. It wasn't an easy journey for Jane, but she continued to move forward as she drew upon new resources to bolster her spirit.

What resources do you have in your life at this time? You don't have to reinvent the wheel to identify resources. It could just be a matter of becoming more aware of what you already have. Use the next sixty seconds to determine which of the following resources could assist you.

PERSONAL

- Family
- Friends and pets
- Coworkers
- Caregivers (doctors, counselors, coaches, ministers, mentors, etc.)

GROUPS

- Church and spiritual affiliations
- Twelve-step groups
- Sports and teams
- School (vocational school, college, continuing education, etc.)
- Social agencies (support groups, food banks, county services, etc.)
- Hobby and special interest groups (book clubs; sewing circles; art, dance, or yoga studios, etc.)

SELF-CARE

- Breathing practices
- Meditation and prayer
- Exercise

- Healthful eating
- Nature
- Upbeat music, books, movies, and TV programs

We all need encouragement to help us through the uncertain parts of our journey. Don't delay. A sustainable and renewable resource may be only a phone call away.

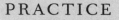

PRACTICE

Make a two-tiered list of sustainable resources. The first category is "High-Priority Resources," what have already proven to be helpful and sustainable. The second category is "Secondary Resources," what will be helpful when a high-priority resource isn't available.

39. Full Presence

*P*resence asks nothing more of us in this next minute than that we experience what is here. In this sense, presence is beyond description and without adornment. Presence is what happens before any filter of thought intervenes. It is pure and without wanting. Presence doesn't judge or attach itself to any event. To be present is to simultaneously enter the realm of the ordinary and the sublime.

The Buddha's teachings in the Samyutta Nikaya Suttas speak to presence, or pure knowing, in verse:

> *In what is seen, there should be just the seen.*
> *In what is heard, there should be just the heard.*
> *In what is sensed, there should be just the sensed.*
> *In what is thought, there should be just the thought.*[34]

Presence doesn't mean we are passive, don't care, or don't possess values of right and wrong. It is not our reactivity and attachment. What people, experiences, and objects make you cringe and pull back? Do you recoil from ugliness, decrepitude, violence, gore? What happens when you encounter that which is desirable, appealing, and beautiful? Do you want to bring it closer, grasp it, possess it? What political perspective, religious belief, worldview do you firmly hold? How do you react to those who hold different views? Presence is not about taking sides or having to be right. It is spacious and impartial. Presence doesn't falter or lose focus. It is the awareness of feelings, sensations, and thoughts as they unfold in any situation. The more often we are present, the more undaunted we are by whatever arises.

To cultivate presence, we authentically and intimately enter into this moment and whatever it brings to our door. As you read this, do you find you are self-critical or self-satisfied with your idea of presence? That would be yet another thought filter you witnessed in the moment. How present are you with the people in your life? How can you bring more openness and availability into each relationship? Can you set your prejudices, conditioning, and need for control aside for a single minute?

Presence also means peering deeply into the true nature of impermanence and change, without resisting. Look and you will notice that everything around you was once something entirely different. The adult was once a child, the wooden table was once a tree, the glass you drink from was once a molten material. No form will remain forever in its present form. When we refuse to accept this fact, disappointment and suffering are sure to find us. Change means letting go and finding compassion for ourselves and others when we hold on to the past. This is the wisdom of presence.

We introduce receptivity into our lives with presence. Receptivity gives others the space to be seen and heard, to be genuine and truthful with us. Presence transforms the next minute. It softens the hardened clay of reactivity into an awareness and a clarity that are alive and dynamic.

PRACTICE

For this one-minute practice with presence, find a quiet place to sit. This is an eyes-wide-open, ears-wide-open, body-wide-open, and mind-wide-open exercise. Once you have settled in, take a couple of diaphragmatic breaths. As you breathe, bring your awareness entirely to the breath, and as you observe it, internally say, "So, this is the way my breath is." You are not trying to change anything; you are being fully open to the breath as it is.

Next, look around your surroundings. If you see something that is pleasing, notice that. You may have a pleasant memory about a person, a picture, a pet, or an object. When this occurs, internally say, "So, this is how my mind thinks about that," or "So, this is how I feel about that." If an emotion such as sadness arises when you think about how one day this pleasing object or person will be gone, internally say to yourself, "So, that's the way it is with impermanence."

Let yourself sit and notice in a neutral and impartial way. Just be present and open. This is a practice that can help you bring presence into even difficult situations. You won't need to run from them but will be able to directly confront what is in the here and now.

40. Create Your Island of Peace

*H*ow often have you heard the word *terror* or the term *war on terror* in the past week? It is hard to find peace when we live in the middle of a war. With television, radio, and newspapers, war and other messages of doom and gloom are brought into our homes. How do you let the news affect your attention? I'm advising not that we cut ourselves off from the world but that we exercise some control over stimuli that cause the brain's stress center to react. In *Rewire Your Brain*, psychologist John Arden makes the case that "sometimes you need a dose of detachment to move yourself beyond negative thoughts and emotions.... Avoid tear-jerker dramas, because they promote a tearful mood. ...Do everything that you can to promote the thoughts, perspective, and behaviors that kindle a positive mood."[35]

Creating a boundary around negative programming is a strategy that works. It made a big difference for Wendy, a forty-year-old who came to see me because of hopelessness, depression, and ruminating thoughts. I soon learned that she worked out of her home and spent most of her free time reading and blogging on websites that were, as she put it, "highly critical and political." When Wendy became more aware of how her avid participation on these sites increased her negativity, she agreed to limit her blogging. Within a few weeks, she felt more upbeat and positive.

How would limiting your exposure to the news make a difference in your life? Of course, the greatest island of peace exists in our own minds, but the point here is to nurture the tranquility that exists within by taking a few simple steps to create peace in your home, your workplace, and even your car. Notice the difference it makes when you apply one-minute mindfulness to the following areas.

Sound has a profound effect on mood. Right now, become aware of the sounds that fill your space as you read. Which sounds are within your control, and which aren't? When I visit my parents, for example, the television is usually turned up so loud that I notice my body tense up, and I become edgy. There have been times when I have gone into another room to steep myself in a few minutes of quiet. What choices can you make to help yourself find a moment of silence, a break from sound?

How we structure our meals has a lot to do with promoting a sense of either intimacy with or disconnection from others. Do you eat with the TV turned off? Are time and space given to express gratitude and to share life stories? Are there ways to beautify the eating area and to make the experience memorable?

Colors, pictures, and other objects can bring beauty and serenity into your living space. Psychologists study colors and know, for example, that shades of green and blue promote feelings of calm. How do the colors in your work and living spaces affect you? What objects or paintings soothe? Is there enough natural light?

Clutter and congestion can contribute to feelings of discomfort and disorganization. Right now, look around your environment to take inventory of the level of clutter. You can also do a mental inventory of any other environment you inhabit. How does the present degree of organization, or the lack of it, affect your mood? Sometimes you may not be able to control all aspects of your environment because of other factors, children and roommates, for example. In such a case, could you create a clutter-free zone in even one part of your shared space?

Use the practice below to add a few grains of peace to your day.

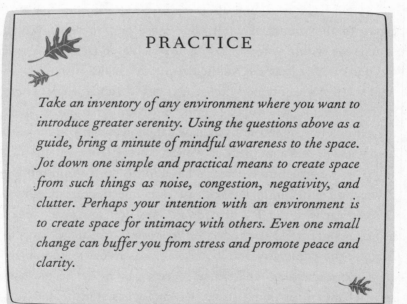

PRACTICE

Take an inventory of any environment where you want to introduce greater serenity. Using the questions above as a guide, bring a minute of mindful awareness to the space. Jot down one simple and practical means to create space from such things as noise, congestion, negativity, and clutter. Perhaps your intention with an environment is to create space for intimacy with others. Even one small change can buffer you from stress and promote peace and clarity.

Part 5

One-Minute Mindfulness for

NATURE, SPIRITUALITY, AND CONTEMPLATION

With one-minute mindfulness, you can find a sense of wholeness and emphasize your spiritual values in the next sixty seconds. A contemplative, reflective approach to each minute welcomes such experiences as humility, learning from the natural world, and cultivating your own voice of wonder, wisdom, and maturity. To enter this path is to hold the entire world in a huge embrace.

41. Contemplating Humility

*H*umility illuminates the deepest core of what it means to be human, how we are all frail and subject to error and how each of us is dependent upon the web of life into which we are interwoven. What this means for each of us is that eventually, like it or not, we will be cracked open and rendered vulnerable and naked by life. I am reminded of a concert I attended recently, where poet and songwriter Leonard Cohen performed. Before breaking into his song "The Bells," he eloquently spoke a few of the song's lyrics, alluding to the light that shines through the imperfect and cracked parts of ourselves.[36]

Being cracked open is not the same as being broken or enduring a Humpty Dumpty moment, unable to put ourselves back together. Neither does humility imply that we are weak and incapable. Leadership expert John Baldoni insightfully writes, "Humility is acceptance of individual limitations — I cannot do it alone — coupled with a sense of resolve to do something about it — I will enlist the help of others. That is the essence of leadership."[37] One-minute mindfulness helps the light of humility and growth shine through the cracks.

Nature has much to teach us about letting our collective

human humility shine through in a way that protects shared resources. With humility, we can accept that we are part of nature, not separate from it or destined to master it for selfish reasons. Today more than ever, we need humility to help us restore harmony and to find sustainable ways of living on the planet. Conceit and arrogance must be cracked open in order for humility to emerge and make a difference in all areas of our lives, from the personal to the global.

Joseph, a thoughtful and compassionate 38-year-old college professor, was struggling with the frustration of making personal choices to benefit the earth. Agitated and anxious, he told me that he and his wife were expecting a third child. "I find it unethical and environmentally unsound," he said with alarm. "There are now seven billion people on the planet, and even the most mindful American consumes a frightening amount." Joseph believed he was failing at what he understood as his larger social responsibility. In our discussion, I learned that he did all he could to live responsibly and leave a light footprint. Over time, Joseph accepted his human desire to have the child his wife was carrying. Instead of focusing on the negatives of bringing another child into the world, he decided to take a leadership role and teach others about the environment, beginning with the sustainable lifestyle he was modeling for his own children. Joseph found a way to let the light shine through his human frailty.

Take a minute to be mindful with the questions below as they guide you on a humble and mature path.

- What mistakes have I made, and what lessons in humility do they hold?
- How can I begin to learn about humility and resilience from nature?
- How might I find more time to spend in nature to help

me better understand humility and my interdependence with the natural world?

- How do my behaviors as a consumer respect or disrespect nature?
- How can I use my flaws to become a leader with compassion and integrity?
- How can I demonstrate to others that we're all in this together?
- How can I remember that my humility is a strength?

PRACTICE

When you forget trying to be perfect, you become present to the way you are and the way things are — cracks and all. For this practice, make a one-minute mindful choice today to let the light shine through something that is not perfect. It could mean that you let go of egocentric behavior in some way or that you think differently about how to consume or how to act toward another. What's also valuable is that with this choice you are acknowledging your imperfect self as you move yourself, others, and the planet forward with greater sensitivity and clarity.

---

42. Finding Silence

Silence is that little, often ignored signpost directing us to return home. It invites a return to abiding peace and equanimity. Silence is not nothingness but the stillness from which clarity and insight can spring. In a culture so loud that it's often almost impossible to think and reflect, silence is feared. No wonder: silence plants the seeds of deeper awareness, questioning, and contemplation. Silence offers nothing less than a revolution of our inner being.

When I first met Bethany, she suffered from an eating disorder and exercise behavior that were exacting a toll on her life and her family. Though painfully thin, she pushed herself like a drill sergeant at basic training camp. She woke up before sunrise for a grueling two-hour regimen of exercise that left her exhausted day after day. Bethany was unwilling to enter an eating disorder treatment program, but she did agree to a ten-day silent Vipassana retreat. *Vipassana* is a Pali word from northern India for what has become known in the West as Insight Meditation. Insight Meditation encourages our capacity to see reality as it is, without adornment. The silent sitting that Bethany did during the retreat caused her to confront her mind. She discovered that her thoughts were not as concrete and substantial as she had thought, and this allowed her to take them less seriously. As it turned out, Bethany cut back on her exercise and started to sit in silence each morning. Though she still struggles with her thoughts and exercise, she courageously continues to use silence to uncover more self-compassion.

The thoughts the mind generates can produce various states of confusion and delusion. Poet and philosopher John O'Donohue wrote, "Perhaps Nature senses the longing that is in us, the restlessness that never lets us settle. She takes us into the tranquility of her stillness if we visit her. We slip into her quiet contemplation and inhabit for a while the depth of her ancient belonging.... When your heart is confused or heavy, a day outside in Nature's quiet eternity restores your lost tranquility."[38] Nature offers us a refuge from our difficult states of mind.

For one minute, let's set aside these pages, those things that are unfinished, memories of yesterday, and other preoccupations so that we can enter into silence. Read the rest of this paragraph before you begin. Keep in mind that in this context, silence is about entering spaciousness. It doesn't mean that having thoughts during this next minute is a failure — far from it. Let yourself step in a new direction without expectation. To support you in this one minute of mindful silence, enlist the help of nature. Find any landscape, natural path, shrub, or tree-lined parking lot or even a potted plant or flower to observe. Sit with your back straight, comfortable but alert. Take some calming breaths and set an intention to be present with nature and its silence. As much as your mind may chatter, simply accept this and return your attention to nature. You might even focus by internally saying, "Resting in nature's silence," or just "Silence, silence." Begin now.

Silence is a process. The more you rest in it, the more its healing tranquility will pave a path to your door.

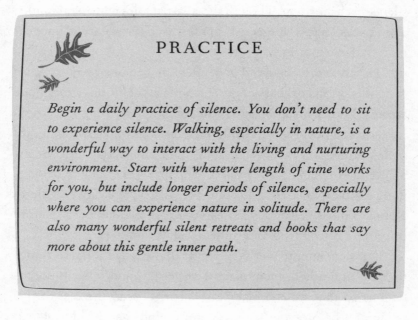

PRACTICE

Begin a daily practice of silence. You don't need to sit to experience silence. Walking, especially in nature, is a wonderful way to interact with the living and nurturing environment. Start with whatever length of time works for you, but include longer periods of silence, especially where you can experience nature in solitude. There are also many wonderful silent retreats and books that say more about this gentle inner path.

43. Beginner's Mind

*B*eginner's mind is open and curious. It does not easily get stuck in dogma; instead, it enters the realm of unlimited possibility. With beginner's mind, we unpack all the empty rules, obligations, and beliefs that occupy countless minutes of our days. Without this extra weight, we can more readily approach any circumstance or person with a sense of awe, suspense, and wonder. With one-minute mindfulness, we may even begin to connect the repeating patterns and dots of coincidence that blossom in our lives.

Imagine this scenario for a moment: If you had no previous learning or conditioning, how would you enter into the next minute? How would you participate in the moment arising before you now?

I am reminded of the story of a Buddhist monk from another country who, shortly after coming to America, made his first visit to a large grocery store. He had no preconceptions of what to expect. Overwhelmed by the abundance of food on the shelves, he immediately began walking through the aisles and blessing all the food. A beginner's mind led him to embrace the experience with gratitude. He saw a measure of abundance that would benefit others.

Many of us make the mistake of viewing situations and persons in a fixed way, like objects, which is limiting for many reasons. For example, we fail to see who is really before us at this moment in time when we see others through a shorthand set of mental criteria, such as their financial status, political views, religion, sexual orientation, education level, and so forth. Beginner's mind releases such judgments and allows a fresh perspective in which each new minute arising in the flow of consciousness is understood to be affecting everyone, including ourselves, in a dynamic experience.

One-minute mindfulness is about jumping into the river of consciousness and intention. When you enter a room, bump into someone you know, and share a laugh at the proverbial water cooler, that is your immersion in this flowing river of experience. You are not separate from it. Beginner's mind facilitates your full participation and awareness in the flow of the moment. Deepak Chopra describes the opportunities that become available to us when we participate with life in this way: "If you catch coincidences at the moment they occur, you are better positioned to take advantage of the opportunities they may be presenting.... The more attention you give to coincidences, the more likely they are to appear, which means you begin to gain greater and greater access to the messages being sent to you about the path and direction of your life."[39]

One minute of mindfulness with the following questions will encourage you to explore what blocks you from participating in the flow with a beginner's mind.

BLOCKAGES TO THE BEGINNER'S MIND

- What places, persons, and situations make me more reactive or fixed in my viewpoint?

- What past experiences and conditioning continue to produce negative emotional states, such as fear, anger, and envy, which prevent me from entering the flow of the next minute?

OPENING TO THE BEGINNER'S MIND

- When do I recall experiencing a childlike openness, wonder, joy, or love, which was my capacity for beginner's mind? Seeing Santa for the first time? My first puppy? My first love?
- How might I interact and flow in an open and curious way?

In its most profound sense, beginner's mind offers freedom from the limitations of the ego and its suffering. May you cocreate and participate fully in the next minute. How sublime!

PRACTICE

Beginner's mind is your flower of consciousness. You can cultivate its blossom in the next minute by noticing the times when you react to your environment and to others in a fixed and limited way. Each time this happens, remind yourself to participate instead with the following words: Let go and enter the flow.

44. Lessons from the Earth

*T*he earth is one of our greatest teachers, offering its valuable lessons for free. All we have to do to be admitted to this perennial school is pay attention. There are lessons on every conceivable subject, including the arts, the sciences, economics, psychology, and the understated and apparently elusive subject of common sense. To learn from the earth, you need only to spend time with it, as you would with anything or anyone you wanted to know more about.

Education writer Michael Schneider asks us to recognize the archetypes of nature that surround and inspire us. In *A Beginner's Guide to Constructing the Universe*, he writes, "Why should the sites of stone temples and wonderful cathedrals be more sacred than a rocky desert or concrete city street if we bring holy consciousness to each of them?...A surprising amount of the world's religious art and architecture has been designed using the timeless symbolic patterns of nature and number....All this was understood in ancient times and deemed so important that it was built into the culture on every level."[40] Schneider provides numerous examples of how archetypal shapes and structures are replicated throughout nature, as well as being reflected in our most revered architectural forms. Imagine: the neurons in our brains resemble the branches of trees!

So, how can you start, in the next minute, to tap into what this sacred school has to offer? For one thing, you don't need to be a scientist, architect, or mathematician. You can begin simply by unplugging from the electronic world and stepping into the nonvirtual one. The digital realm may teach you something about nature and even inspire you to care more, but it cannot immerse you in nature's innate wisdom in the same way that sitting in a wood or gazing out at the ocean can. A stroll out your door may be all that's required.

Let's suppose you happen upon a tomato plant, or that you have decided to grow tomatoes. While the idea of growing a tomato might seem like child's play, it takes a tremendous amount of care, knowledge, and time to turn seeds into seedlings and then into a mature plant with ripe red fruit. Tomato plants need direct sunlight, warmth, and space to branch out. Without enough space, regular watering, and proper drainage, they won't thrive. The tomato fruit also needs protection because it is part of the diet of many birds and animals. If a simple tomato teaches anything, it is that patience and care are necessary for any idea, life change, goal, or desire we hold. Long before a particular goal starts to take shape, the seed of that thought needs to be protected from criticism or misunderstanding so that it has enough time to take root in fertile ground.

During my contemplative workshops, I have participants walk outside to observe nature's ever-changing aliveness, its shapes, colors, and designs. Whatever challenge you may be facing, you can use the next minute to gain valuable insight from nature. The following three steps help clarify how you can do this.

1. Determine what qualities, resources, or both would help your life most at this moment. More time, flexibility, strength, peace, evenness of temper, love, money?

2. Once you have settled on what you are looking for, set the intention to have nature teach you what you must do in order to get what you need.

3. Spend some uninterrupted, unscripted time in nature, whether in a park, a forest, your backyard. Don't force anything during this time. Let go of the expectation of finding an answer, and just be present with childlike wonder. If you don't find what you're looking for, don't give up. Good things take time, like any maturing seed.

PRACTICE

Cultivate an attitude of respect and awe for the natural world. Mindfulness of the environment means that in this next minute you recognize your relationship with the earth and make a decision to show that you care about this relationship. As captivating as technology may be, only by appreciating nature's timeless form and wisdom will we move forward with care and compassion for the earth that supports our well-being.

45. Gazing at the Sky and the Moon

The sky and the moon are waiting for your gaze. Their spaciousness invites us to a revolutionary perspective, the big view, the right now. To gaze at the sky and the moon is to leave the thinking, discursive, calculating, judging mind behind and to expand our awareness beyond the limited self to vast consciousness, of which we are an integral part. Stargazing and moongazing do not have to be an escape from the mundane; instead, they can be a way to grasp that the ordinary is also sublime when we become fully present to it.

The practice of gazing at the sky and the moon brings two important things into focus. First, it lets us embrace wholeness and unity, balancing out our personal, limited, and separate view of existence. British philosopher and Zen practitioner Alan Watts described this well when he said, "You're breathing. The wind is blowing. The trees are waving. Your nerves are tingling. The individual and the universe are inseparable, but the curious thing is, very few people are aware of it. Everything in nature depends on everything else. So it's interconnected.... When you look out of your eyes at nature happening out there, you're looking at you."[41]

After all, any definition of you or me as a separate individual must naturally take into account all the things around us that are not us. Isn't it true, for example, that your identity as a father or a mother, a child, a lover, an employee, an entrepreneur depends entirely on relationship, not you alone? You even have a relationship to your body, your thoughts, and your emotions. Gazing at the cosmos catapults us into the truth of the bigger view, where we are an interconnected and essential part of all things.

Second, gazing — whether at the sky, the moon, or the wall in your office or living room — is an eyes-wide-open practice that cultivates naked awareness in its purest form. The key is to stay with the openness, the vastness of mind and awareness. When the nineteenth-century Tibetan Buddhist lama Jamgön Kontrül Lodrö Thayé taught a version of skygazing, he advised, "Let it remain naturally. Don't spoil it by manipulating, by controlling, by tampering with it, and worrying about whether you are right or wrong, or having a good meditation or a bad meditation. Leave it as it is, and rest your weary heart and mind. The ...absolute truth is nothing other than the very nature of this uncontrived, ordinary mind. Don't look elsewhere."[42]

Now it's time to start gazing. Begin by getting settled in your body. Assume a natural position, and center the body, sensing it fully, from the tips of your toes to the top of your head. If there is emotion, tension, or tightness anywhere, don't try to escape it; just notice it. Next, settle into your breathing, letting it be unforced, just as it is. Notice the breath's natural flow. Finally, settle into your mind — fantasies of the future or memories of the past — however it happens to be. Now, cast your gaze outward upon the vast emptiness, maintaining moment-to-moment awareness. Let your eyes look upward and outward and above the horizon. Be as present to your thoughts, bodily sensations, and breath as you are to the spaciousness before you. Take it all in and be free.

You can gaze at the sky anytime, even for a minute, to find balance. This practice can take you from an ego's-eye view to a bird's-eye view of things in an instant. Here you find freedom from expectation and craving because nothing is other than it is supposed to be. Over time, you may even notice how you — the observer — and the sky, the moon, and so forth — the observed — become woven together as one.

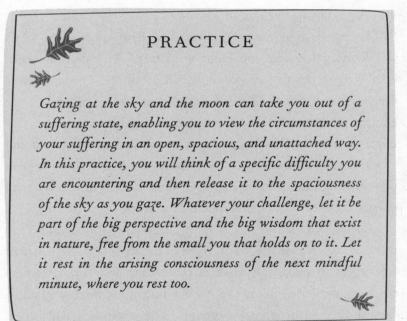

PRACTICE

Gazing at the sky and the moon can take you out of a suffering state, enabling you to view the circumstances of your suffering in an open, spacious, and unattached way. In this practice, you will think of a specific difficulty you are encountering and then release it to the spaciousness of the sky as you gaze. Whatever your challenge, let it be part of the big perspective and the big wisdom that exist in nature, free from the small you that holds on to it. Let it rest in the arising consciousness of the next mindful minute, where you rest too.

46. Be the Change

*T*he word *volunteer* originally came from an ancient Latin word, *voluntarius*, meaning "voluntary." To volunteer, then, is to exercise our free choice on behalf of others. The act of volunteering influences how we design our lives and makes our choices more conscious and meaningful. Volunteering also signifies generosity, a cherished form of spiritual development and expression in all traditions. To volunteer is to offer up the fruit of our enlightened intention. It elevates us and others by both deepening connection and reducing suffering.

Gandhi challenged us with his powerful statement, "You must be the change you want to see in the world."[43] We can wait for others to make the world a more sane and compassionate place, or we can volunteer to use the upcoming minute to move mindfully in a beneficial direction. The compassionate action you take in the next minute does not have to once and for all create world peace, end all injustice, or otherwise dramatically alter the world — it only has to be one action that can serve such ideals. Many people hold back from helping because they wrongly believe that their actions would be inadequate to make the huge changes that are needed. They mistakenly judge what they can do as a failure.

With a one-minute mindfulness approach, you can engage in the process of contributing to the change you want to see manifested at large. Reflect on the following question: Do I hold back from volunteering because I believe my help will not be enough, just a drop in the bucket? I like to use the example of Mother Teresa, who committed one small voluntary act of kindness, then another, and then another. Ordinary acts of service accumulate into an inspiring, indelible, and loving declaration about the power of helping one another. Have you been on the sidelines, secretly wanting to serve? Whatever has kept you from participating in the past, one-minute mindfulness can give you the focus right now to alter your life and make that difference, just as Mother Teresa did.

Right now, think of someone you admire who helps others with their gifts of energy and enthusiasm. This can be someone on the world stage or the neighbor who bakes cookies for a fundraiser. When you volunteer, you come into concert and harmony with others. If you have been blessed with good fortune, volunteering is an opportunity to give back. If you struggle, volunteering can take you out of your situation and help you discover how good it feels to help others. Every day, look for one-minute mindfulness opportunities by keeping these questions in mind:

- How can I volunteer right now? What knowledge, skills, energy, or resources can I share now?
- Who is making a contribution right now that I admire? How could I do the same?
- If I were brave, courageous, and fearless in the next minute, what commitment to volunteering would I make?

As you work on being the change you want to see in the world, remember that service can also be expressed to benefit the earth and all its creatures.

PRACTICE

Keep a journal about your journey of volunteering. Using one-minute mindfulness, look for opportunities to volunteer throughout the day, and keep track of these. You can act on them in the moment or reflect on taking a long-term approach in a particular area. Volunteering opens your heart, so listen to your heart to guide you to those areas where you feel a connection — such as working with children, the sick, the underprivileged, the elderly, the disabled, and so forth. Share your dreams of volunteering with others, and you may gain new insights and extra encouragement.

47. Embracing Contemplation

*C*ontemplation has played a defining role throughout human history. When French philosopher René Descartes penned the famous words *Cogito ergo sum* — I think, therefore I am — he might just as easily have written, "I contemplate, therefore I am." Although contemplation commonly refers to an act of thoughtful consideration, it is actually a process of exploring deeper levels of being, awareness, and meaning.

Contemplation is derived from the Latin word *contemplum*, which means "to create space for observation and interpretation." Creating such space is the first essential step in preparing the mind, the body, and the spirit for an opening in awareness. Religious and spiritual traditions have long applied a variety of methods for emptying and transforming the ordinary mind. The use of song and vibration to transform the ordinary mind goes far back to Hinduism's four-thousand-year-old Gāyatrī Mantra. Resting in the presence of God through centering prayer and the reading of sacred scripture are long-standing Christian contemplative practices. The whirling dervishes of Sufism use ecstatic dance and movement to enter contemplative states. Meditation and mindfulness practices, which we explore in this book, also shift conscious awareness into more sublime contemplative states. When the mind is transformed in this way, we allow it to move into a place of prayerful awareness and attention.

In his book *Open Mind, Open Heart*, Father Thomas Keating writes, "Contemplative prayer is a way of tuning in to a fuller level of reality that is always present and in which we are invited to participate. Some suitable discipline is required to reduce the obstacles to this expanded awareness. One way is to slow down the speed at which our ordinary thoughts come down the stream of consciousness."[44] When our minds are nervous and jumpy, like an untamed horse, it is difficult to enter contemplative space.

Contemplation is not only the sacred domain of philosophers, theologians, and academicians. An attitude of devotion and openness can be brought to our daily practices and experiences as well:

- our emotions and the emotions of those around us
- how we interact with others
- our relationship with nature and our spirituality
- meaning found in scripture, poetry, literature, films
- sharing observations and interpretations with others in an open way
- our breath and our thoughts
- art and beauty
- the process of change, learning, and listening

You can prepare your mind for a contemplative state by using any of the practices presented earlier, such as walking (chapter 12), focused breathing (chapter 14), and using a calming word (chapter 35). You can also set the intention in that pivotal "next minute" to enter a contemplative place by using the following affirmation:

May I center and calm the weary mind.
May I be fully open, present, and available.
May I open to this next precious minute.
May I be at peace, ever mindful and contemplative.

PRACTICE

Give yourself the gift of contemplation to open more deeply to your inner life. Include some contemplative reading, as described here, along with another practice that speaks to you. Give yourself at least five to ten minutes to spend with a passage of scripture or a beloved poem.

When you first settle in, state the affirmation above and be clear about your intention to open to a new relationship beyond the written word, which could mean opening to God, your deeper purpose, or your unique path, as the case may be. This is an experience of opening; it is received rather than taken. Let go of expectations and be willing to accept whatever experience may come — boredom, transcendence, anger, forgiveness, and so forth. Now you are ready to begin reading. Hear the words as if they were written just for you. Notice if a particular word, line, or shorter passage happens to draw you in. Then recite that word or passage. As you do this, try not to analyze, but just sit with the truth of what is revealed.

Eventually, this experience may prompt you to add a few more minutes to rest in contemplative reading or another form of reflection. Throughout the rest of your day, you will find that this practice will make it easier to step into a contemplative state in the next minute whenever you choose to do so.

48. Pray for What You Already Have

*T*he next minute is not what we think it will be — not even close. But it can be what we decide to focus on. If we constantly look for what's missing from our lives — that big house, dream car, perfect relationship, ideal job — then the upcoming minute might be filled with regret, remorse, sadness, frustration, and hopelessness. If we consistently appreciate what is currently before us and available in our lives — the car that runs, the roof over our head, the job that provides resources, and the relationships we do have, most importantly with ourselves — then we spare ourselves disappointment.

I was running a workshop when I met Hannah, a 50-year-old nutritionist, and one of the topics was overcoming depression through gratitude. During the break, Hannah approached me, held out her right arm, and pointed to a bracelet adorning her wrist. Dangling from the bracelet were all the letters of the alphabet. She proceeded to tell me the story behind this bracelet. For years she struggled with depression and anger because of a highly stressful job and some unhealthy relationships. Antidepressants had come and gone, but nothing seemed to work. By the midpoint of her life, Hannah, by her own admission, was not a pleasant person to be around. She could have just shut down; instead, she placed her faith in bringing gratitude to what was already in her life. This shift gradually and dramatically altered her experience of the stream of minutes that followed. Hannah smiled as she told me, "The change was so obvious that people at work asked me if I was taking medication. I think they were hoping it was something they could take." To stay connected to her practice of gratitude, Hannah uses her bracelet and a journaling exercise in which she chooses a different letter of the alphabet and records all the things she's grateful for that begin with that letter.

I'm not suggesting you ignore the ruts in your life by covering them up with chocolate frosting. That would leave you with a chocolate-covered rut. But at the same time, the rut is not all there is. Would you agree that this very minute the path is also paved and can be navigated without driving over the ruts? This is within our control. To understand where you are placing your awareness and to recognize the ruts, take the following one-minute mindfulness inventory.

WHAT IS MISSING

- Do I tend to focus on what I don't have? If so, how is this affecting my relationships?
- What do I think is missing in my life?
- How do I feel when I place my awareness on what's missing?

WHAT IS PRESENT AND AVAILABLE

- What is present and available to me?
- How can I begin to redirect my awareness to the gifts I have?

- How does looking at what is in my life make me feel? Does it give me hope and energy?
- How will feeling this way affect my relationships?

I am reminded of the film *Under the Tuscan Sun*, in which the heroine, played by Diane Lane, moves to Italy after her divorce. The things she wishes to have in her life — people to cook for, a family, and a wedding — manifest in such unexpected ways that she doesn't immediately recognize that they are present. When her realization dawns, she glows with peace, joy, and wholeness.

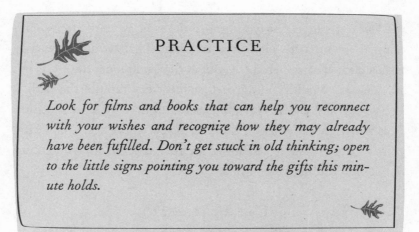

PRACTICE

Look for films and books that can help you reconnect with your wishes and recognize how they may already have been fufilled. Don't get stuck in old thinking; open to the little signs pointing you toward the gifts this minute holds.

49. Know Your Seasons

*T*he seasons change effortlessly, without prompting. They don't need to be instructed: *Okay, winter, you've been lounging around long enough. It's time to wake up and make room for the spring rains. And you, spring, you better step aside and give summer a chance to produce growth and activity. Remember, summer, to slow down for fall or else you'll wear yourself out, and there won't be a harvest and time to regroup.* Just as an apple tree knows how to grow and produce fruit, our lives move with the wisdom and purpose of their own seasons. This innate wisdom is ours to access in the next minute of mindfulness.

Psychiatrist Henry Emmons advocates attuning to these seasons through careful attention to our sleep, exercise, and nutrition: "Just a few generations ago, most people lived much closer to the earth.... Farmers and other rural people lived in harmony with the rhythms of nature, working longer hours in the summer and 'hibernating' in the cold, punishing winter."[45] The body's cycles are important to recognize and so are the critical junctions in our life cycle — the times when we need to pause and the moments when we need to hit the restart button.

Seasons exist in all areas of our lives. Relationships, for example, begin with a honeymoon phase, filled with all the hope and dreams of a new spring. New jobs are a spring, as are new puppies, new cars, and new years. This doesn't mean that we can't find spring in the midst of an existing relationship or job, but identifying the season can help us know when it's time to regenerate or rest.

Bring a few minutes of mindfulness right now to examining your life cycle and the seasons you are experiencing in different areas of your life. You may want to write down your responses.

- Significant Relationships
- Friendship
- Work or Livelihood
- Important Project(s)
- Age, Energy, and Physical Self-Care
- Wisdom
- Forgiveness
- Life Purpose and Goals
- Volunteerism and Generosity
- Emotional Growth
- Spiritual Growth
- Self-Compassion and Acceptance

This is by no means a complete list, and it's not intended to provoke self-criticism. Even if you are not where you would like to be, that's just an indication of the current season. Each season is really a journey of change and growth in preparation for another season; no season is an all-defining end point. Now, use one-minute mindfulness to answer the questions that follow to give you more insight into your seasonal journeys.

- What is one thing you learned by identifying your seasons?
- Which areas in your life are asking you to pause for rest and regeneration?
- Which areas help you appreciate your progress and effort?
- In which areas are you ready to move on to another season?

May you continue to tap into the wisdom of the seasons as needed in each new minute.

PRACTICE

Using the work you did above, choose one season that you would like to see progress into the next cycle. Look for examples among your friends and others who have successfully made such a shift. Remember to stay in the minute-by-minute process. Seasons don't instantly change; they take time. Deeply appreciate the season you are in, even as you move toward a new one.

50. Send Messages of Peace

Our words and actions can bring anxiety, despair, and fear into the world, or they can inspire faith, hope, and love. Which do you choose? When our words and deeds convey peace, they create a very real sense of serenity and safety for others. When we communicate peace outwardly — through our tone, body language, and action — we simultaneously illuminate our inner being with the light of repose and calm.

Gandhi understood the magnitude of peaceful conduct when he wrote, "Always aim at complete harmony of thought and word and deed. Always aim at purifying your thoughts and everything will be well. There is nothing more potent than thought — deed follows word and word follows thought. The world is the result of a mighty thought, and where the thought is mighty and pure, the result is always mighty and pure."[46] The old adage "Sticks and stones can break my bones, but words can never hurt me," is false, even in brain science. For example, recent studies show that verbal abuse is both psychologically damaging — increasing the likelihood of depression, anxiety, and anger — and damaging to the brain.[47]

To choose peace in the next sixty seconds is a profound act.

How can we start to change old patterns and attune our being and brain to peace? Gandhi had such a prescription for the spiritual community he established in India. They incorporated several prayers for peace from other traditions to demonstrate their respect for persons of all faiths. Here are excerpts from just a few of those peace prayers. (All the prayers that were used are posted online.)[48]

Be generous in prosperity and thankful in adversity.
Be fair in thy judgment and guarded in thy speech.
—— Bahai peace prayer

Give us the wisdom to teach our children to love,
to respect and to be kind to each other
so that they may grow with peace of mind.
—— Native American peace prayer

Blessed are the peacemakers,
for they shall be known as the Children of God.
—— Bible, Matthew 5:9

I earnestly wish that the wind will soon blow away
all the clouds hanging over the tops of the mountains.
—— Shinto peace prayer

Let understanding triumph over ignorance,
let generosity triumph over indifference,
trust triumph over contempt, and Truth over falsehood.
—— Zoroastrian peace prayer

Centering our awareness on peace primes our mind and being for tolerance and acceptance of others. This means not that we permit abuse but that we act from a place of peace and love, even while standing firmly against abuse. This is another kind of power, the constructive power of love, and it asserts peace and spiritual growth. Centering our awareness gives us the ability to impact the world through one-minute mindfulness. Centering our being on peace is the first step to living in peace. How healing and "one-derful"!

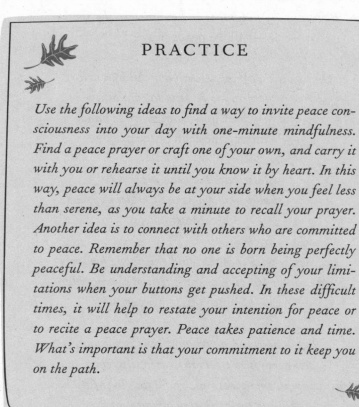

PRACTICE

Use the following ideas to find a way to invite peace consciousness into your day with one-minute mindfulness. Find a peace prayer or craft one of your own, and carry it with you or rehearse it until you know it by heart. In this way, peace will always be at your side when you feel less than serene, as you take a minute to recall your prayer. Another idea is to connect with others who are committed to peace. Remember that no one is born being perfectly peaceful. Be understanding and accepting of your limitations when your buttons get pushed. In these difficult times, it will help to restate your intention for peace or to recite a peace prayer. Peace takes patience and time. What's important is that your commitment to it keep you on the path.

Acknowledgments

My heartfelt appreciation extends to all those individuals throughout history who have dedicated themselves to sharing the peace-promoting teachings of mindfulness with others. I thank my late teacher, the Venerable U Silananda, who was a tireless mindfulness guide to seekers; Ashin Thitzana, a spiritual monk brother for whom I am eternally grateful; U Thondara and the monks and community of the Burma Buddhist Monastery; Randy Fitzgerald, a wonderfully talented writer and friend whose kind and generous sharing of ideas and feedback helped shape this work; Greg Crosby, a friend, intuitive encourager, and one-minute mindfulness worker who shares his immense gifts with others; Robert Biswas-Diener, for sharing his important work in the field of happiness; Lama Surya Das, who always reminds me that humor is an innate great perfection; my fellow board members of The Center for Mindful Eating, for their great heart and support as well as their extraordinary efforts toward reducing suffering in the world; Georgia Hughes, editorial director at New World Library, for her wonderful insights and enthusiasm for this project; Marc Allen, for his vision to make a positive change in the world and for sharing his story, inspiration, and experience; Bill Gladstone, my agent, for his wholehearted support of this project; and Kristen Cashman from New World Library and copyeditor Vesela Simic, for their editorial gifts, which have enhanced these pages. Also, my thanks extend to numerous others — including friends, teachers, colleagues, clients, acquaintances, students, and so on — with whom I had the pleasure of exploring and learning more about mindfulness. I am also deeply grateful to my family's generous spirit — my siblings, Jim and Cynthia; my parents, Barbara and Norman, who forever amaze me with their resilience, support, and love. My deep gratitude goes to Sanda for always encouraging my journey into mindfulness, even during challenging times. May all beings step onto this peaceful path, and together may we continue to awaken and heal in this next minute.

Notes

1. John O'Donohue, *Beauty: The Invisible Embrace* (New York: Harper Perennial, 2005), p. 29.
2. Ananda Maitreya, *The Dhammapada* (Berkeley, CA: Parallax Press, 1995), p. 18.
3. Sharon Salzberg, *Loving-Kindness: The Revolutionary Art of Happiness* (Boston: Shambhala, 1995), p. 131.
4. Martin Buber, *I and Thou* (New York: Scribner, 1970).
5. Rick Hanson, *Buddha's Brain: The Practical Neuroscience of Happiness, Love & Wisdom* (Oakland, CA: New Harbinger, 2009), p. 41.
6. Donald Altman, *The Mindfulness Code: Keys for Overcoming Stress, Anxiety, Fear, and Unhappiness* (Novato, CA: New World Library, 2010).
7. Robert Emmons and Michael McCullough, "Counting Blessings versus Burdens: An Experimental Investigation of Gratitude and Subjective Well-Being in Daily Life," *Journal of Personality and Social Psychology* 84, no. 2 (2003): pp. 377–389.
8. Shunryu Suzuki, *Zen Mind, Beginner's Mind*, ed. Trudi Dixon (Boston: Shambhala, 2010), p. 1.
9. Shahrad Taheri, Ling Lin, Diane Austin, Terry Young, and Emmanual Mignot, "Short Sleep Duration Is Associated with Reduced Leptin, Elevated Ghrelin, and Increased Body Mass Index," *Public Library of Science, Medicine* 1, no. 3 (December 2004): pp. 210–217.

10. Ensar Becic, Gary Dell, Kathryn Bock, Susan Garnsey, Tate Kubose, and Arthur Kramer, "Driving Impairs Talking," *Psychonomic Bulletin & Review* 17, no. 1 (February 2010): pp. 15–21.

11. "Driven to Distraction: New Study Shows Driving Hinders Talking," *Science Daily*, January 25, 2010, http://www.sciencedaily.com/releases/2010/01/100122222222.htm (accessed November 15, 2010).

12. Søren Kierkegaard, *The Parables of Kierkegaard*, ed. Thomas Oden (Princeton, NJ: Princeton University Press, 1989), p. 27.

13. Glenn Clark, *The Man Who Tapped the Secrets of the Universe* (St. Paul, MN: Macalester Park Publishing, 1988), p. 27.

14. Martin Seligman, *Learned Optimism: How to Change Your Mind and Your Life* (New York: Pocket Books, 2006), p. 80.

15. Roz Shafran and Warren Mansell, "Perfectionism and Psychopathology: A Review of Research and Treatment," *Clinical Psychology Review* 21, no. 6 (2001): p. 901.

16. William Fielding Ogburn, *Social Change with Respect to Culture and Original Nature* (Ithaca, NY: Cornell University Library, 2009; originally published 1922), p. 280.

17. *Teachings of the Buddha*, ed. Jack Kornfield, trans. Bukkyo Dendo Kyokai (Boston: Shambhala, 1996), p. 96.

18. Alex Linley, Janet Willars, and Robert Biswas-Diener, *The Strengths Book: Be Confident, Be Successful, and Enjoy Better Relationships by Realizing the Best of You* (Coventry, UK: CAPP Press, 2010), p. 146.

19. Frank Coppieters, *Handbook for the Evolving Heart* (Marina del Rey, CA: CONFLU:X Press, 2006), p. 194.

20. Lewis Mehl-Madrona, *Coyote Wisdom: The Power of Story in Healing* (Rochester, VT: Bear & Company, 2005), pp. 16–17.

21. Donald Altman, *Mindful Eating Meal Cards: Friendship Field* (Portland, OR: Moon Lake Media, 2007), Blessings Card no. 48.

22. Robert Louis Stevenson, *The Letters of Robert Louis Stevenson* (Volumes 1 & 2) (Fairford, UK: Echo Library, 2006), p. 75.

23. Jack Kornfield, *The Wise Heart: A Guide to the Universal Teachings of Buddhist Psychology* (NY: Bantam Books, 2008), p. 346.

24. Viktor Frankl, *Man's Search for Meaning* (Boston, MA: Beacon Press, 2006).

25. Pavel Somov, *The Lotus Effect: Shedding Suffering and Rediscovering Your Essential Self* (Oakland, CA: New Harbinger Publications, 2010), p. 5.

26. Judi Bopp, Michael Bopp, Lee Brown, and Phil Lane Jr., *The Sacred Tree: Reflections on Native American Spirituality* (Twin Lakes, WI: Lotus Press, 2004), p. 66.

27. Bhante Henepola Gunaratana, *Eight Mindful Steps to Happiness* (Somerville, MA: Wisdom Publications, 2001), p. 14.

28. Patt Lind-Kyle, *Heal Your Mind, Rewire Your Brain* (Santa Rosa, CA: Energy Psychology Press, 2009), p. 77.

29. Susan Albers, *50 Ways to Soothe Yourself without Food* (Oakland, CA: New Harbinger Publications, 2009), p. 109.

30. John Ratey and Eric Hagerman, *Spark: The Revolutionary New Science of Exercise and the Brain* (NY: Little, Brown and Co., 2008), p. 4.

31. Brian Clement, *Hippocrates LifeForce: Superior Health and Longevity* (Summertown, TN: Healthy Living Publications, 2007), p. 57.

32. Center for Science in the Public Interest, "Sugar Intake Hit All-Time High in 1999," CSPI Newsroom, http://www.cspinet.org/new/sugar_limit.html (accessed December 17, 2010).

33. "Thought for Food: Imagined Consumption Reduces Actual Consumption," *Science Magazine* 330, no. 6010 (December 10, 2010): pp. 1530–1533, http://www.sciencemag.org/content/330/6010/1530 (accessed December 17, 2010).

34. Peter Strong, *The Path of Mindfulness Meditation* (Denver, CO: Outskirts Press, 2010), p. 116.

35. John Arden, *Rewire Your Brain: Think Your Way to a Better Life* (Hoboken, NJ: Wiley, 2010), pp. 52–53.

36. Leonard Cohen, in concert, Rose Garden, Portland, OR, December 8, 2010.

37. John Baldoni, *Lead by Example: 50 Ways Great Leaders Inspire Results* (New York: AMACOM, 2009), p. 194.

38. John O'Donohue, *Eternal Echoes: Celtic Reflections on Our Yearning to Belong* (NY: Harper Perennial, 2000), pp. 15–16.

39. Deepak Chopra, *The Spontaneous Fulfillment of Desire: Harnessing the Infinite Power of Coincidence* (New York: Three Rivers Press, 2003), p. 27.

40. Michael Schneider, *A Beginner's Guide to Constructing the Universe: The Mathematical Archetypes of Nature, Art, and Science* (New York: Harper, 1995), pp. xxii–xxiii.

41. Alan Watts, "The Real You," http://www.youtube.com/watch?v=mXmz605GAnc (accessed March 7, 2011).

42. Jamgön Kontrül Rinpoche, "View and Meditation of the Great Perfection," as quoted by Lama Surya Das, "Sustaining Present Awareness," http://www.dzogchen.org/teachings/talks/Sustain Aware10694.html (accessed December 21, 2010).

43. Ed Shapiro and Deb Shapiro, *Be the Change: How Meditation Can Transform You and the World* (New York: Sterling, 2009), p. 10.

44. Thomas Keating, *Open Mind, Open Heart: The Contemplative Dimension of the Gospel* (New York: Continuum, 1997), p. 37.

45. Henry Emmons with Rachel Kranz, *The Chemistry of Joy: A Three-Step Program for Overcoming Depression through Western Science and Eastern Wisdom* (New York: Fireside, 2006), p. 92.

46. Mahatma Gandhi, *The Way to God: Selected Writings from Mahatma Gandhi* (Berkeley, CA: North Atlantic Books, 2009), p. 36.

47. Martin Teicher, Jacqueline Samson, Yi-Shin Sheu, Ann Polcari, and Cynthia McGreenery, "Hurtful Words: Association of Exposure to Peer Verbal Abuse with Elevated Psychiatric Symptom Scores and Corpus Callosum Abnormalities," *American Journal of Psychiatry* 167 (December 2010): 1464–1471.

48. Unity.org, "Gandhi's Peace Prayers from the World Religions," http://www.unity.org/homepageArchive/features/gandhis PeacePrayers.html (accessed December 27, 2010).

Bibliography and Resources

BOOKS

Altman, Donald. *Art of the Inner Meal: The Power of Mindful Practices to Heal Our Food Cravings.* Portland, OR: Moon Lake Media, 2002.

——. *Living Kindness: The Buddha's Ten Guiding Principles for a Blessed Life.* Portland, OR: Moon Lake Media, 2003.

——. *Meal by Meal: 365 Daily Meditations for Finding Balance with Mindful Eating.* Novato, CA: New World Library, 2004.

——. *The Mindfulness Code: Keys for Overcoming Stress, Anxiety, Fear, and Unhappiness.* Novato, CA: New World Library, 2010.

Arden, John. *Rewire Your Brain: Think Your Way to a Better Life.* Hoboken, NJ: Wiley, 2010.

Baldoni, John. *Great Communication Secrets of Great Leaders.* New York: McGraw-Hill, 2003.

——. *Lead by Example: 50 Ways Great Leaders Inspire Results.* New York: AMACOM, 2009.

Beattie, Melody. *Gratitude: Affirming the Good Things in Life.* New York: Ballantine, 1992.

Begley, Sharon. *Train Your Mind, Change Your Brain: How a New Science Reveals Our Extraordinary Potential to Transform Ourselves.* New York: Ballantine, 2007.

Bohm, David. *On Dialogue.* London and New York: Routledge, 1996.

Bopp, Judi, Michael Bopp, Lee Brown, and Phil Lane Jr. *The Sacred Tree: Reflections on Native American Spirituality*. Twin Lakes, WI: Lotus Press, 2004.

Buber, Martin. *I and Thou*. New York: Scribners, 1970.

Chödrön, Pema. *Start Where You Are: A Guide to Compassionate Living*. Boston: Shambhala, 2004.

Chopra, Deepak. *The Spontaneous Fulfillment of Desire: Harnessing the Infinite Power of Coincidence*. New York: Three Rivers Press, 2003.

Chozen-Bays, Jan. *Mindful Eating: A Guide to Discovering a Healthy and Joyful Relationship with Food*. Boston: Shambhala, 2009.

Church, Dawson. *The Genie in Your Genes: Epigenetic Medicine and the New Biology of Intention*. Fulton, CA: Elite Books, 2009.

Clark, Glenn. *The Man Who Tapped the Secrets of the Universe*. St. Paul, MN: Macalester Park Publishing, 1988.

Clement, Brian. *Hippocrates LifeForce: Superior Health and Longevity*. Summertown, TN: Healthy Living Publications, 2007.

Coppieters, Frank. *Handbook for the Evolving Heart*. Marina del Rey, CA: CONFLU:X Press, 2006.

Diener, Ed, and Robert Diener. *Happiness: Unlocking the Mysteries of Psychological Wealth*. New York: Wiley, 2008.

Durston, Diane. *Wabi Sabi: The Art of Everyday Life*. North Adams, MA: Storey Publishing, 2006.

Easwaran, Eknath. *The Mantram Handbook: Formulas for Transformation*. Petaluma, CA: Nilgiri Press, 1977.

Emmons, Henry, and Rachel Kranz. *The Chemistry of Joy: A Three-Step Program for Overcoming Depression through Western Science and Eastern Wisdom*. New York: Fireside, 2006.

Frankl, Viktor. *Man's Search for Meaning*. Boston: Beacon Press, 2006.

Gandhi, Mahatma. *The Way to God: Selected Writings from Mahatma Gandhi*. Berkeley, CA: North Atlantic Books, 2009.

Gunaratana, Bhante Henepola. *Eight Mindful Steps to Happiness: Walking the Buddha's Path*. Somerville, MA: Wisdom Publications, 2001.

Hanson, Rick. *Buddha's Brain: The Practical Neuroscience of Happiness, Love & Wisdom*. Oakland, CA: New Harbinger, 2009.

Kabatznick, Ronna. *The Zen of Eating: Ancient Answers to Modern Weight Problems*. New York: Perigree Trade, 1998.

Keating, Thomas. *Open Mind, Open Heart: The Contemplative Dimension of the Gospel*. New York: Continuum, 1997.

Kierkegaard, Søren. *The Parables of Kierkegaard*. Edited by Thomas Oden. Princeton, NJ: Princeton University Press, 1989.

Kirsten Daiensai, Richard. *Smile: 365 Happy Meditations*. London: MQ Publications, 2004.

Kornfield, Jack, ed. *Teachings of the Buddha*. Translated by Bukkyo Dendo Kyokai. Boston: Shambhala, 1996.

———. *The Wise Heart: A Guide to the Universal Teachings of Buddhist Psychology*. New York: Bantam, 2008.

Lind-Kyle, Patt. *Heal Your Mind, Rewire Your Brain: Applying the Exciting New Science of Brain Synchrony for Creativity, Peace and Presence*. Santa Rosa, CA: Energy Psychology Press, 2009.

Linley, Alex, Janet Willars, and Robert Biswas-Diener. *The Strengths Book: Be Confident, Be Successful, and Enjoy Better Relationships by Realising the Best of You*. Coventry, UK: CAPP Press, 2010.

Mahasi, Sayadaw. *Fundamentals of Vipassanā Meditation*. Berkeley, CA: Dhammachakka Meditation Center, 1991.

Maitreya, Ananda. *The Dhammapada*. Berkeley, CA: Parallax Press, 1995.

Mehl-Madrona, Lewis. *Coyote Wisdom: The Power of Story in Healing*. Rochester, VT: Bear & Company, 2005.

———. *Healing the Mind through the Power of Story: The Promise of Narrative Psychiatry*. Rochester, VT: Bear & Company, 2010.

Nhat Hanh, Thich. *The Miracle of Mindfulness: An Introduction to the Practice of Meditation*. Boston: Beacon, 1987.

O'Connor, Richard. *Undoing Perpetual Stress: The Missing Connection between Depression, Anxiety, and 21st Century Illness*. New York: Berkley Trade, 2006.

O'Donohue, John. *Beauty: The Invisible Embrace*. New York: Harper Perennial, 2005.

———. *Eternal Echoes: Celtic Reflections on Our Yearning to Belong*. New York: Harper Perennial, 2000.

Ogburn, William Fielding. *Social Change with Respect to Culture and*

Original Nature. Ithaca, NY: Cornell University Library, 2009. Originally published 1922.

Ratey, John, and Eric Hagerman. *Spark: The Revolutionary New Science of Exercise and the Brain.* New York: Little, Brown and Co., 2008.

Salzberg, Sharon. *Loving-Kindness: The Revolutionary Art of Happiness.* Boston: Shambhala, 1995.

Schneider, Michael. *A Beginner's Guide to Constructing the Universe: The Mathematical Archetypes of Nature Art, and Science.* New York: Harper, 1995.

Schwartz, Jeffrey, and Sharon Begley. *The Mind and the Brain: Neuroplasticity and the Power of Mental Force.* New York: ReganBooks, 2002.

Schwartz, Jeffrey, and Rebecca Gladding. *You Are Not Your Brain: The 4-Step Solution for Changing Bad Habits, Ending Unhealthy Thinking, and Taking Control of Your Life.* New York: Avery, 2011.

Seligman, Martin. *Learned Optimism: How to Change Your Mind and Your Life.* New York: Pocket Books, 2006.

Shapiro, Ed, and Deb Shapiro. *Be the Change: How Meditation Can Transform You and the World.* New York: Sterling, 2009.

Silananda, Venerable U. *The Four Foundations of Mindfulness.* Boston: Wisdom Publications, 1990.

Somov, Pavel. *The Lotus Effect: Shedding Suffering and Rediscovering Your Essential Self.* Oakland, CA: New Harbinger Publications, 2010.

Stevenson, Robert Louis. *The Letters of Robert Louis Stevenson* (Volumes 1 & 2). Fairford, UK: Echo Library, 2006.

Strong, Peter. *The Path of Mindfulness Meditation.* Denver, CO: Outskirts Press, 2010.

Surya Das, Lama. *Awakening the Buddha Within: Tibetan Wisdom for the Western World.* New York: Broadway Books, 1997.

———. *Buddha Standard Time: Awakening to the Infinite Possibilities of Now.* New York: HarperOne, 2011.

Suzuki, Shunryu. *Zen Mind, Beginner's Mind.* Edited by Trudi Dixon. Boston: Shambhala, 2010.

Whybrow, Peter. *American Mania: When More Is Not Enough.* New York: Norton, 2006.

WEBSITES

Donald Altman's websites: www.oneminutemindfulnessbook.com and www.mindfulpractices.com and www.mindfulnesscode.com

Antihunger and antipoverty organizations: http://www.bread.org/learn/links.html

The Center for Mindful Eating: www.TCME.org

Center for Mindfulness and Psychotherapy: www.mindfulnessandpsychotherapy.org

Center for Mindfulness in Medicine, Healthcare, and Society: www.umassmed.edu/content.aspx?id=41252

Dana Foundation: www.dana.org

Hope Foundation: www.hopefoundation.org

Laboratory for Affective Neuroscience: http://psyphz.psych.wisc.edu/

Network for Grateful Living: www.gratefulness.org

Social Cognitive Neuroscience Laboratory, UCLA: www.scn.ucla.edu

Unity: www.unity.org

Index

About the Author

*D*onald Altman, MA, LPC, is a practicing psychotherapist, former Buddhist monk, award-winning writer, and board member of The Center for Mindful Eating (TCME.org). He is an adjunct professor at Lewis and Clark College Graduate School and is on the faculty of the Interpersonal Neurobiology program at Portland State University.

Donald conducts mindful living and mindful eating workshops and retreats around the nation and is known as America's Mindfulness Coach for the way he makes mindful living and spiritual values accessible in daily life. Donald trained with the Venerable U Silananda, author of *The Four Foundations of Mindfulness*, at a Buddhist monastery located near the San Bernardino Mountains in Southern California. He is a member of the Burma Buddhist Monastery Association.

A prolific writer whose career spans more than thirty years, Donald has written for children's television and documentaries and has had numerous articles appear in print. An avid motorcyclist, Donald enjoys riding along the Oregon coast. He lives in Portland, Oregon.

NEW WORLD LIBRARY is dedicated to publishing books and other media that inspire and challenge us to improve the quality of our lives and the world.

We are a socially and environmentally aware company, and we strive to embody the ideals presented in our publications. We recognize that we have an ethical responsibility to our customers, our staff members, and our planet.

We serve our customers by creating the finest publications possible on personal growth, creativity, spirituality, wellness, and other areas of emerging importance. We serve New World Library employees with generous benefits, significant profit sharing, and constant encouragement to pursue their most expansive dreams.

As a member of the Green Press Initiative, we print an increasing number of books with soy-based ink on 100 percent postconsumer-waste recycled paper. Also, we power our offices with solar energy and contribute to nonprofit organizations working to make the world a better place for us all.

Our products are available
in bookstores everywhere.
For our catalog, please contact:

New World Library
14 Pamaron Way
Novato, California 94949

Phone: 415-884-2100 or 800-972-6657
Catalog requests: Ext. 50
Orders: Ext. 52
Fax: 415-884-2199
Email: escort@newworldlibrary.com

To subscribe to our electronic newsletter, visit
www.newworldlibrary.com

	HELPING TO PRESERVE OUR ENVIRONMENT			
3,183 trees were saved	New World Library uses 100% postconsumer-waste recycled paper for our books whenever possible, even if it costs more. During 2011 this choice saved the following precious resources:			
	ENERGY	WASTEWATER	GREENHOUSE GASES	SOLID WASTE
www.newworldlibrary.com	22 MILLION BTU	600,000 GAL.	750,000 LB.	200,000 LB.

Environmental impact estimates were made using the Environmental Defense Fund Paper Calculator @ www.papercalculator.org.